FAITH - COURAGE - GRACE

When Giving Birth Doesn't Go as Planned, You Find a Way to Live

JACQUIE A. MCIVER

FOREWORD BY TIM ROSS

Bible quotations are taken from: KING JAMES VERSION Scripture quotations marked (KJV) are taken from the King James Version. Public Domain

NEW LIVING TRANSLATION

Scripture quotations marked (NLT) are taken from the New Living Translation, copyright © 1996, 2004, and 2015 by Tyndale House Foundation. Used by permission of Tyndale House Publisher, Inc. Carol Streams, Illinois 60188. All rights reserved.

ISBN: 979-8-9868643-0-3 (Paperback)
ISBN: 979-8-9868643-1-0 (e-book)

Cover design: CW Technology Consulting, LLC
Interior book design: The Rod Hollimon Company
Editorial services: Nzadi Amistad Editing and Writing Services
Back cover photo: Invision Light Photography
Hair Stylist: Hair by Toni Striblen

Strategic Mind Productions, LLC
Lewisville, Tx 75067

Printed in the United States of America

Dedication

This book is dedicated to my mother, Nettie B. McIver. Before she left for her eternal home, she would always encourage me to keep God first. Her famous saying was, "Thank God for the good days and the bad ones, as well." Mom would always say, "We must trust God with our lives." Thank you, Mom, for your loving and continued support. I cherish every moment we had together. Thank you for loving your grandson, Jeremiah, no matter what he faced in life.

Table of Contents

Acknowledgments

Writing this book encompasses many other wonderful people that the Lord has brought into my life. Some were there before the birth of Jeremiah, and many came along this journey. With heartfelt appreciation and gratitude, I thank those who connected with me on this journey when Jeremiah entered the world.

To the fantastic medical team at the Medical City at Lewisville and the beautiful families like Sherry & Mario Gouge. Our children shared a room during Jeremiah's stay in the NICU, and we prayed together many days and nights. I personally want to say "thank you" to the incredible Dr. LaKeitha Foster Truehill, as God used her outstanding medical skills to ensure that Jeremiah remained here on earth. Thank you to the phenomenal group of nurses who worked in the NICU during that time.

I have met some sensational therapists along this journey, but I would be remiss if I didn't thank Michelle Purcell, DPT, for providing outstanding physical therapy to Jeremiah. Since he was seven months old, she has been with Jeremiah and is still helping him along this journey.

The Lord always knows what you need before you even know, and He knew that I would need someone to walk closely beside me to help care for Jeremiah. He brought me the most precious and beautiful gift in the person known as my goddaughter, aka "daughter", Iesha Liles. Jeremiah is blessed to have her as his big sister. Her loving mother, Shannel Hall, did not hesitate to share Iesha with me as we all walk along this journey as a family. I am forever thankful to God for bringing us all together. I am also very thankful that God has given me an older sister and one that I am not biologically connected to. However, she has been there with me and continues to support me, and she encourages me to do whatever God places on my heart. Thank you to my older sister, Valerie Walker Michaux.

I am grateful for the many people that have become my support team, and each one has brought so much joy to our lives. It is a blessing when it comes to having ministry leaders who open their hearts and show God's steadfast love toward my family and me. Thank you to my pastor and friends, Tim and Juliette Ross.

I am especially grateful for my beta-reading team, which helped to bring this book to life. Thank you,

Mary Blue, Karla Jackson, and Donnette Ward.

Finally, this book would not have come to fruition without the outstanding mentorship of my dear sister and friend, Elaine R. Penn. She believed in the vision for this book and in me as a person. She was also a part of my beta-reading team. I am sincerely grateful for her tireless efforts to ensure that I brought life to the story that was within me. Thank you for everything.

Thank you to every person who has ever supported us with any kind of acts of kindness or demonstrations of genuine love and for embracing the various changes along this journey. We appreciate you all.

Foreword

I have known Jacquie A. McIver for quite a while, and I know her to be a woman of strength, character, and integrity. Upon these pages, you will find a story unlike any other. For in it, there is transparency, vulnerability, determination, conviction, and grace, an immeasurable amount of grace. You will soon find out that this story is not just feel good.

Jacquie takes you through highs and lows, mountaintops and valleys, care, concern, triumph, and tragedy. And in these ebbs and flows, in these ups and downs, what you will find and feel is God's grace displayed in yet another extravagant way to prove how much He is with us, for us, and what He means to us.

My prayer, as you read these words on these pages, is that you will allow this story to change your life. Let it not be said that you were not given the opportunity to go on a journey. Let it not be said that you were not given an opportunity to be challenged. Let it not be said that you were not given an opportunity to grow. Let it not be said that you were not given an opportunity to throw away your excuses.

I invite you to allow the strength, the grit, the determination, the weakness, the frailty, and, once again, the grace that God has given to Jacquie to now be given to you. This book starts to change your life as soon as you turn this page.

Tim Ross, Founding Pastor

Embassy City Church

Irving, Texas

Introduction

Being in trouble can reveal to you who God truly is. The honesty shared during a walk with God helps with a better understanding of life, especially when life happens. We don't always like it when we don't fully understand certain things that happen in life. We ask the question, "Why did this have to happen to me?" Many times, we have the faith to believe in something or someone greater than ourselves, but we don't always have an answer for why difficulties occur.

I have been a Christian since I was a child, but my walk with God didn't truly begin until the day my life changed forever. The birth of my child demonstrates the power of God that is always with us, no matter what happens. What does it mean to become a believer or to be born-again?

For me, it was growing up in the church and learning about who God is and what He has done. Life can transform you, giving you a level of intimacy with God that you never thought you would ever experience. After faithfully attending church and actively participating in church activities, it is ironic for me to say that

I did not know God until my son came into this world.

I was very familiar with who God was and what He had done. Prior to the birth of my son, I was actually serving as an executive pastor and had been spreading the word of God for years. I recognize that you can teach about the word of God by studying it and then sharing it with others.

However, experiencing God takes everything to a different level of intimacy. Many people would equate this to being saved, allowing God to be Lord over your life. In other words, totally submitted and surrendered to God, no matter what happens. It is my hope that this book will help you grow to another level of closeness with God.

Your life can change in an instant. Sometimes, that change can seem very painful, yet it may end up being the best thing that ever happened to you. That is an oxymoron because who can ever say that they like pain? That statement was not intended to misdirect you into believing that I like the pain; instead, it was meant to demonstrate that pain has a purpose in everyone's life. It is always what you do with the pain that makes the difference.

We all have and will experience pain or challenging circumstances in life, and we must learn how to walk through them. Don't ever let what's happening to you cause you to think that you are not valuable. Truthfully, some things can happen to you that will shake you to the very fiber of your being. This is not to minimize what you have experienced or are currently experiencing in your life. This is to let you know that, no matter what has happened or what will happen, you should never give up on life. As long as you have breath, you have hope. This is an essential ingredient for life. You have to keep hoping, despite how hard things might become or even feel.

Let's be clear. What happens to us can change our lives and the directions of our lives. It serves a significant purpose, and it is the one thing that is shaping my life and helping me discover my God-ordained purpose. Who would have ever thought that a devastation would birth a genuinely new way of life? My ordinary life transformed into a purpose-driven life because of one decision.

As you read this book, you will glean a lot of truths and learn how to regroup after your world is turned upside down. I never thought my life would turn in this direction until I took a few moments and looked at where I am. Interestingly enough, I am not even where I am supposed to be, but just one step closer on my journey. Honestly, the experiences described in this book are genuine and authentic. I believe that they will positively impact your life and help you to keep moving forward, no matter what happens in your life. You must read this book with an open mind, so you don't miss the life lessons that can transform you and others from pain to purpose.

What used to be my usual was redefined by one decision. It may not seem like much, but for those of you who are believers in Jesus Christ, you may think that this following statement couldn't possibly be accurate. However, one's decision to sin can create a life-changing moment that results in a closer walk with God. Don't get caught up in the word *sin*; instead, see the underlining meaning with each step on the journey.

Let me be the first to say, sin is wrong, no matter what; however, God has a way of taking our mess-ups and turning them into His original purpose. When you are in the midst of things, it does not seem that way, nor does it feel that way. You will learn quickly that the word of God is so sincere, no matter who you are and where you have been in life: "And we know that God causes everything to work together for the good of those who love God and are called according to his purpose for them" (Romans 8:28 NLT).

God has a way of transforming what you deem the worst thing you could ever do into something beautiful. All I know is, if you are facing a challenge that is beyond your control, why not take a few steps back and examine what God is saying to you through it?

Even if you are the perpetrator of the activity, still ask God to show you His purpose and plan, so you will receive the courage to keep on living. Everyone who belongs to God has opportunities to create something new, as long as they focus on what He is saying to them directly. As you read this book and acknowledge the pain inside of you, you should look at this as an opportunity to experience strength through adversity.

A critical thing that has come out of my pain is that, no matter what I have done and no matter how low I may have felt about what I did, God's love never changes. He is committed to us, no matter what. This is one critical thing to keep in mind as you continue reading and learning more about *faith, courage, and grace*.

Being transparent, I always show my genuine emotions, but I never stay in negative emotions; instead, I work my way through. Working through those emotions through God and with God's help is the inspiration behind this book. When it gets tough and you don't know what steps to take, lean on your **faith** and walk in **courage** each day while experiencing the pure **grace** of God. After reading this book, you will be uplifted and will have the confidence that you, too, will make it through and see many victories along the way. You will also learn that faith is a way of life, and it is real.

Part 1

Chapter 1

Bad Faith News

Have you ever made a life decision that hit you to the core of your soul, and you just didn't know what to do? Well, I have. Let me share with you a little bit about my decision.

At the age of forty-two, I decided to get pregnant. My biological clock was ticking, and the thought of not having a child was heartbreaking, especially after living a healthy life and knowing the only concern my doctors had was my age.

After I became pregnant, my doctors gave me specific instructions, and I followed them to the tee. I ate the right foods and kept my stress level under control. Of course, because I was forty-two, my health care providers took every precaution possible to ensure that my baby would be healthy. Pregnancy brought such great joy, and month after month, the thoughts of a new future were becoming a reality. Creating a list of things needed for the baby was a big priority. As the weeks passed and the delivery date got closer, I thought, the baby will soon be born, and items must be in place. The birth of my baby was on the horizon.

Being a mother-to-be is the best stage of life because you live with the expectation of delivering a healthy baby; it is a simple example of faith. I prepared my mind with thoughts like, I'll be caring for someone who lived inside of me. That thought brought tears to my eyes.

My pregnancy was reasonably good and uneventful, with the only challenge being having morning sickness a little longer than usual. The doctors, however, never seemed concerned about this. I was eating the right foods and taking my vitamins...yeah, those huge ones the doctor prescribes. It was the doctors' and my goal for me to be healthy and for the baby to be born healthy.

As I was about to enter my third trimester, life felt good. I was already thanking God for the glorious day that I would give birth to a beautiful little boy. Unfortunately, that's not exactly what happened.

One day, I stood up from my recliner chair and felt a rush of water run down my leg. I cried out to my baby's father and said, "I can't stop going to the bathroom."

He said, "Your water broke."

I shouted at him, "What do you mean?"

I immediately had him call 911 because of the fear of what was happening to my baby. When the ambulance arrived, they rushed me off to the nearest hospital. I was at week twenty-seven, and my water had just broke. I had no clue what was about to happen. The only focus was wanting my baby to be born alive and healthy.

Once I arrived at the ER, hearing the doctors talking about what to do with the nurses was scary. While they were collaborating with each other, I was praying to God. I heard them say to me that my baby and I were at high risk. You should have seen the look on my face. It was a look of completely oblivious shock. All I knew at the time was I needed to remain calm. That didn't last too long because I started crying and couldn't stop. Tears came streaming down my face. The nurses came over to console me and to let me know that they would ensure that my baby and I were all right. Just for a brief moment, the crying stopped, but it was only long enough for me to reply, "Okay." Then, the tears kept coming profusely.

Moments passed by, and nothing was being said about the next steps or what was even happening. I didn't know if they had determined if my baby was healthy enough to survive since there was lots of water lost. With the new technologies and medicines available today, they were confident that they could save us both. Upon hearing this, my heart, mind, and spirit called out to the Lord. I needed His help, and I needed it right now!

Calling out to the Lord with great passion was necessary during this time. Not understanding what was happening made me feel helpless. Watching the medical team moving at such a rapid pace around me heightened my nerves. That was a very dark moment that exposed the need for a heartfelt cry and a plea to God.

Often, before a crisis happens, we think we know how we will respond. We believe that we will be calm and in control. Unfortunately, it is not until we face a challenging situation that is out of our control that we find out what we will do.

Medical Team's Decision

The doctors came to my bedside and informed me that my baby was too small to survive if they delivered him that day. Immediately, I asked, "What are our options?"

In the midst of my fear and sadness, they replied with optimism. They stated that there was a medication they could give me to help my son's lungs grow. However, this medication had several side effects that could negatively impact me. Boy, the list was very long. In my head, my thoughts were racing to the Lord, asking for my baby to live. After listening to the laundry list of side effects and understanding the dangers, I agreed to take the medication. After ingesting the medicine, they wanted me to take it easy for seventy-two hours.

Wow! I thought. The doctors didn't lie when they said this medication had some consequential side effects. One of the most noticeable side effects was having hallucinations. I didn't know what they were until I experienced them for those seventy-two hours. I honestly thought I was losing my mind. Confusion became real, and so was the uncertainty of seeing things that weren't necessarily present. My body felt very heavy, and getting up out of bed was not an option. They wanted me to be still, so the medicine could fully work. Those seventy-two hours felt like an eternity. Deep down in my heart, my only thoughts were of wanting my baby to have the opportunity to live.

During this time, the hospital I was admitted to couldn't provide the best care. They had limited services and weren't equipped to handle an emergency like mine. They were considered a level-one hospital, and I needed to be admitted to a level-three facility. The levels determined the services they could offer a patient based on their needs. The doctors knew that my child would be born early and that he needed to be at a hospital with a level-three NICU (Neonatal Intensive Care Unit).

After receiving the medication, they transferred me to another bed that would be placed in an ambulance. Then, the transfer from one hospital to another took place. The ride is a faint memory. All I remember is that, when my eyes opened, my room looked a whole lot different. Truthfully, I was not sure if this was a hallucination or reality. The most important thing happening in my subconscious was wondering if this medicine was helping my baby. God and time were the only things that knew the outcome.

When the seventy-two hours were over, it took a little bit for the medication to wear off. Actually, it took over twenty-four hours to feel some type of normalcy. After coming back to myself and my good consciousness, that was when it became clear that my room had changed. I hit the red button to call the nurse into the room, so I could ask her about my current location. She looked at me for a moment with confusion. A light bulb must have gone off in her mind when she realized the medication was leaving my body. She then shared with me that I was at the Medical Center of Lewisville with a big smile. It was great to hear about my new location because it was a familiar place.

I was in a private room. Not having a roommate made a huge difference because I didn't want anyone to hear me crying throughout the day. I had been admitted on a Sunday, taken the seventy-two-hour medication, and then woke up on a Wednesday, wondering, How is my baby? Can you imagine all the thoughts that were going through my head? Let me share a few — Is my baby still alive? Will he be able to survive in my stomach until week thirty-five? If he's not in an amniotic sac, will he even live? If he is born, will he be healthy or have difficulties? Is God mad at me?

Yes, that thought entered my head during this time of crisis. Let's be honest with ourselves; all kinds of thoughts come and go. However, one key lesson is determining which beliefs you are going to let lead your life.

As believers in Jesus Christ, we are taught to pray and not ask God any questions. During this time in my life, however, I asked all kinds of questions. I even asked, "Why are You allowing this to happen?" I felt so many different emotions, such as anger, fear, confusion and, yes, even guilt. Can you guess what the front-runner of my emotions was? If you guessed fear, then you guessed right. I was so afraid of what was going to happen. Even after I prayed about it, fear wouldn't leave me alone.

When I woke up that Thursday, they had opened up the window blinds to let some sunshine in the room. I asked them to close them because, at that very moment, the feeling of joy did not exist within me, so my preference was to keep the room as dark as possible because that was how I felt, that was where my heart and mind were at that time. I was in pain, both physically and mentally, and it felt like there was no right or wrong to my reasoning. The only thing that kept running through my head was, Did the medicine work or not?

Later that night, I started to feel what I thought were gas pains. During a brief discussion with one of the nurses on duty, I mentioned that I had not gone to the bathroom to have a bowel movement. You never know how important it is until you haven't released for five days. The nurses explained that the medication could cause great difficulty using the bathroom. Another question came to mind, so I asked, "Will that negatively impact my baby since he is not in the amniotic sac, which protects him?"

One of my crazy thoughts that occurred was, Is my being backed up smothering my child? I didn't know, so I asked. The one good thing was the nursing team never made me feel weird or strange. The nurses answered every one of my questions with compassion. They did their best to reassure me. They were doing the best they could. Even amid the craziness, God still provides some peace. He had the right team of nurses caring for me during this critical time.

On Friday morning, those gas pains that were discussed previously were back again. The uncertainty of not knowing what was happening with my body didn't make this a good situation. Initially, the plan was to keep me in the hospital until week thirty-five. This would give my baby ample time to grow.

The pains in my stomach were happening at a rapid pace. Now, they were at the point where, whatever medication they were giving me, it didn't help. I still hadn't moved my bowels. And I wondered, How is the baby living outside of the amniotic sac?

The stress of all of this had gotten to me. I was having the biggest meltdown ever. The tears were increasing minute by minute. While the tears were flowing, the pains were increasing. I shouted out to God, "What is happening to me? This is too much for me to handle!" The louder I got, the more the pain increased. Hitting the nurses' button became an every ten-minute thing.

Finally, they decided to place a belt around my stomach that was connected to a medical machine. This would allow the doctors to monitor the baby closer than the other monitor that had already been attached to me. The belt showed so many lines on the monitor that I didn't know what was happening. Panic became my best friend. Not that I wanted it to be, but it happened. In spite of it all, I still prayed and cried out to God. Many times, it was a silent cry. Yet God heard me. It's funny that we think God is hard of hearing. He's not at all.

A fleeting thought came to my mind while all of this was happening. The crying and shouting weren't changing my circumstances at all. As a matter of fact, they hindered many things. I stopped for a moment and spoke to myself, "If you have prayed, then believe God heard your prayers."

I took a deep breath, and immediately, a calmness came over me. It was as if everything was being put together for the following steps to take place. The nurses came into the room and noticed the multiple lines that were displayed on the monitor. An urgent call was made to the on-call doctor to come to my room. It was quite apparent that some things were happening that needed immediate attention. A doctor entered my room, and he proceeded to make a phone call. He asked,

"How long have you been in pain?"

I answered, "Since yesterday."

He stepped away from my bed to make another call. Within fifteen minutes, there were, at least, three different doctors in my room. The thoughts that entered my head were, What in the world is happening that all of these doctors need to be in my room? The head doctor spoke to me and told me what was going on. He explained that the pain wasn't gas; instead, they were contractions. I began to laugh because, all this time, I thought it was gas. In reality, it was my baby moving around in my stomach, trying to get out. Even for the brief moment I laughed, the actual thought was, What is next?

The doctors had the nurses prepare me for an emergency C-section. My baby was about to be born. Once again, the medical team was hurrying around me. This time, I was still scared because I didn't know what would happen with my baby. However, even while being afraid, that calmness didn't leave me. I stopped and said, "Lord, please help me through this."

They asked me to call my family to come to the hospital. I called my pastor, as well. Following those instructions, they arrived and began to gather around in my room. Nobody had a clue about what was happening. Everyone had this look on their faces, as if they didn't know what to say. It was hushed in the place. The only thing I heard were the monitors going off. I simply asked everyone to pray for my baby and me.

It's Baby Time

While rushing me off to the operating room, the doctors explained that they would numb the lower part of my body. I said to myself, "I would hope so, if you plan on doing a C-section." My witty self surfaced, even during this extremely trying time. I knew the doctors were trying to keep me calm by sharing what was about to happen. I asked, "Is my baby all right?"

At that very moment, no one answered me. I waited until we got into the operating room. Repeating my question to the medical team, I asked, "Is my baby all right?"

That was the only thing that mattered at that very moment.

Once they transferred me over to the operating

table, the doctor replied, "We hear his heart beating."

In that very chaotic moment, that was the best answer ever.

They had me move to the edge of the operating table. Then, I was asked to lean forward, touching my chest to my knees. The words "be still and don't move" echoed in the air. Following these precise instructions was one of the most essential things for me to do. If there had been any movement on my part, the situation could have drastically and abruptly changed.

The first needle went in, and they tested to see if my legs were numb. Ironically, the feeling of them touching my legs was very prominent. They had to do another needle in my back. I heard the same instructions and obliged accordingly. The second needle elicited a little better response. However, feeling was still there when they touched my feet. Here we go again with another needle, I thought. Finally, the third needle numbed my lower body.

I was lying down on my back as everything began to take place. Not having any feeling helped calm my nerves. One of the doctors was excellent about telling me everything that he was doing. He made a few jokes, and we all laughed. The laughter helped in that very moment because I couldn't see anything that they were doing.

Interestingly, while I didn't feel any pain, there was a brief moment in which I felt lots of pressure. The doctor opened me up very wide because my son had moved to the upper part of my body. When a baby is not in the amniotic sac, he goes wandering. He was still connected to the umbilical cord, so that meant my son was receiving all the necessary nutrients needed to live.

When they took him out, I heard my son cry. The joy that overtook my mind was unexplainable. It was music to my ears. The sound of a baby's cry is usually the first thing a new parent experiences. In addition to his cry, several doctors and nurses were by my side, and they immediately took my son into their care. No one brought my baby to me because he was too small and fragile. While the doctor was closing me up, he shared that they had put my son in an incubator. The nurses and doctors, then, took my son to the NICU. After the C-section was completed, they moved me to my recovery room to monitor me closely.

Eventually, I was moved back to my room, so I

could continue to rest up. I shared with my family and friends that I'd had a baby boy. They needed to learn about his cry. This was all the information that was relevant at the time. You know, because none of them had ever directly experienced giving birth to a premature baby, the questions started coming, like, Who does he look like? Impulsively, I quickly asked them to please hold all questions. The reason was that they'd never brought him to me to see. In the best voice I could muster while cracking in my throat was taking place, I shared that no one knew what this experience was like. My heart led me to share with everyone that I was nervous because I didn't know what to expect. I said this very gently. Respectfully, I requested that they hold all questions until some additional information was disseminated to me from the doctors.

Some nurses from the operating room came to my bedside and asked if I wanted to see my son. Instantaneously, my response was "yes." They took his father and me downstairs to the NICU. When we arrived, my heart stopped beating because the only vision I saw was a very tiny baby hooked up to every possible mach-ine in the NICU. While my eyes swelled up with tears, the nurses came to my bed and asked if I would be okay. My only response was "hopefully."

While looking at all that was taking place with a mystified facial expression, there weren't many words that I could say. There laid my son with so many needles and tubes attached to him. I had to ask, "Will he live?"

The nurses were very optimistic in their response to me. No longer could I hold back the tears as I gazed upon my son. The look of disbelief was very present. I asked, "How much does he weigh?"

The answer just about floored me. One of the nurses said, "He weighs one pound and fifteen ounces."

I thought, How in the world is my baby going to live? Then, a quiet voice spoke to me. It said, "Everything is going to be all right."

Drying up my tears and removing the shocked look from my face was my personal goal. We left the NICU and headed up to my room, so I could rest. Subsequently, the nurses asked me, "Who do you want to go see your son next?"

My response was, "Take my mother down, along with her friend."

It would have been extremely challenging for me

to see my mother looking at her grandson. When she returned to my room after visiting with my son, she stated that she had never seen anyone that small before. She kissed me on my cheek and shared that everything was going to be all right. Soon after, my mom and her friend left, and the others followed them out.

This birthing experience was one that, if you had told me this would happen, there would be no way I would have believed you. My son, who we named Jeremiah, aka "JD", was in the NICU, literally fighting for his life.

No member of the medical team could explain why things happened the way that they did. They couldn't give accurate responses because they didn't know. I am appreciative to them for not saying things that they thought I wanted to hear. I appreciate them for being as upfront and truthful as humanly possible. Doctors are trained to practice medicine, but that doesn't mean they have all the answers.

The Incubator Life

Jeremiah spent over eighty-five days in the NICU. These were some of the most challenging days of both of our lives. On the night of his birth, while I was in my room recovering from having Jeremiah, a code blue occurred in the hospital. The nurses entered the room to advise me there was to be no movement outside in the hallways. This was standard procedure whenever a code blue occurred. I eagerly obliged because, at that point, they hadn't taken me off the pain medications. I was supposed to be weaned off them the very next day. Then, I would be required to get up and walk.

The night was getting late, and everyone had left my room. Jeremiah was down in NICU, living in an incubator. A nurse entered my room almost every three hours to check my monitors and vital signs. How could anyone get rest or even sleep, for that matter? It was a very long night. As the nurse entered my room, I saw that her eyes were completely red, as if she had been crying. I stopped her and asked, "Are you okay?"

She replied, "Yes, I'm doing fine."

Well, honestly, even a person who couldn't see could tell that something was going on with her. So, instead of me persistently asking her what was wrong, I simply asked her if she would mind if I prayed for her. She looked at me and said, "You just had a baby, and you don't even know how he's doing, yet you want to pray for me."

She proceeded to open up and share what was troubling her at that time. I listened, and then she grabbed my hand, and we prayed. Once again, she had this look as if to say "if you only knew what was really happening." I found out later that the code blue that night was for my son. The doctors' and nurses' priority was to stabilize him and provide him with what he needed at that very moment. And they did.

The nurse left the room looking a little better than she had when she'd entered the room. Ironically, she was my nurse all night. We smiled at each other each time she entered the room. Deep down on the inside, I just wanted to sleep. I was tired after having my baby. I had been tired for a long time. From the time my water broke at twenty-seven weeks, I had been on an emotional roller coaster. The night felt as if it wasn't ever going to end. My thoughts were with Jeremiah as I had no idea how he was doing in the incubator. Honestly, I didn't even know what his little body was feeling at that time. It was one of the scariest nights ever. Who really knew what was happening with my son?

I rolled over in the bed, and there stood one of the medical doctors. She asked me, "Where is your son's father?"

I said, "I sent him home to get some rest."

Strangely, she proceeded to ask, "Where is your pastor?"

I expressed to her that I'd sent everyone home because I was tired. Shock took over my heart, and all I could feel was my heart beating really fast. Then, another doctor came in and asked, "Where is your pastor?"

Whenever a doctor asks for a priest or pastor, you know that there is something very serious happening.

My next thought was, Why do they want to know my child's father's and pastor's locations? She proceeded to share with me that she would like for them both to return to the hospital. Being a new mom and seeing your tiny child whisked off to an incubator, your mind can only do one thing: think the worst. I told the doctor I could call them and ask them to return.

My attempt to ask any questions was muted

because she immediately said she would like to speak with all of us simultaneously. If you have ever experienced that before, you understand that the beating of your heart feels like it wants to stop. All kinds of thoughts entered my mind: What is happening with my baby? Is he still alive?

Yes, being asked to have critical people return to the hospital before a doctor shares information is not always a favorable experience. I understand the doctor only wanted to ensure I had support following whatever information was about to be shared.

The nurses came to ask me if I wanted to go down to the NICU to see my son. My instinct was to go, but my mouth stated that I would wait for his father and my pastor to come. One hour felt like an eternity. That's how long it took for them to arrive.

When they made it to the hospital, the nurses informed the doctor. Then, we all went down to the NICU to see my son. Tears welled up in my eyes because I had never seen anyone so small with so many needles coming from his little body. My son was on his side with all kinds of machines connected to him, yet he looked so peaceful. I felt horrible as I watched my son lying there in that plastic tube. I wanted to hold him and touch him. That is what I dreamt about before becoming a mother. I was frustrated at the fact that I was unable to hold my newborn baby. Everything in me wanted to holler and cry, but I didn't want to cause a scene.

My son had more machine sounds going off, and several nurses were standing by his incubator. They were doing many different things, and I had many questions, but I didn't want to disturb their process.

As a mother, I wanted to know what was happening with my son and why there was so much commotion going on around him. The doctor proceeded to share with us that my son had had two code blues that night and that he was currently breathing on a ventilating system. Immediately, it felt as if someone had punched me in the gut. I began to cry and asked, "What do you mean 'he's breathing on a ventilator'? What happened?" I cried out, "Can someone please explain to me what happened to my son?"

There was no clear, direct response to my question because, honestly, nobody knew. I was traumatized by what was being said, but I wanted to understand the options for my son.

The incubator was about three feet from where I was lying, and I wanted to ensure that my son couldn't hear what was being said. Instantly, my thoughts were, we need to speak life, no matter what. I listened to the doctors and nurses as they talked things over with my son's father. They asked him what he would like for us to do. "Do you want to remove your son from the ventilator? Then, we can see if he will survive."

It was clearly communicated that this was the riskiest option. The other option was to leave him on the ventilator, and they could monitor him to see if anything changed. Hold your breath for the response my son's father gave to the doctors and nurses. He said, "God wants more angels in Heaven." Essentially, he told them that they could remove our son from the ventilator.

Then, the doctors and nurses came to me and shared the same option with me. Before I could respond to their question, I had a question. Since my son's father and I were not married, I wanted to know if he could make a decision on my son's behalf. The nurses turned to the doctors and asked the question. One of the doctors proceeded to share a simple answer with everyone —

"No." The doctor explained that my son's father would have to prove he was the father.

Peace came all over me because my first emotion was not peace at all. My response to their initial question was to keep my son on the ventilator. Can you imagine how unstable my thoughts were during this time? There was an array of different emotions, and they were all over the place. No one could say anything to me for a moment because I couldn't stop crying. I was so devastated in a true transparent moment that I didn't even know if I was coming or going. Sometimes, life can hit you so hard that you may not know how to process everything that is happening.

My son was in his incubator, and they brought me closer to him. A nurse asked me if I wanted to touch him. I responded, "No, not at this time."

I looked over at my son's father with deep hurt and noticed he had fallen asleep. As a woman, I had to ask myself, "Why did I even get pregnant by him?" The vast thoughts overshadowed the moment that I was having because I had lost all respect for him. The hurt was so bad it took me a few hours before I could stop crying. My tears were from hurt, anger, disappointment, and pure love for my son. I mustered enough strength to ask my pastor to stand on the opposite side of my son's incubator so that he could pray. He laid his hand on the incubator and prayed a mighty prayer. The nurse came back to me and asked if I wanted to hold Jeremiah. I repeated the same answer as before — "No." The nurse looked at me strangely, but I knew, deep down on the inside, my son was going to live. She proceeded to explain in a voice that had so much hesitation that she thought it would be good if I touched him. Of course, I was still on pain medication, but I could hear my heart saying not to fear. The nurse wanted me to know that they didn't believe Jeremiah would live until the next morning. I said to her and the rest of the NICU staff, "Can you take me back to my room? And I will come down to see Jeremiah in the morning."

All I knew was that God had heard my and my pastor's prayers and that He was going to help me through this entire situation. I believed with all of my heart that Jeremiah would live and not die. It was my faith in action.

Transformation Night

They took me back up to my room on my bed, and I proceeded to ask everyone to go home. I didn't want to talk to anyone. All I wanted was to be left alone. If you could think of the highest roller coaster ever, my emotions were even higher than that. In all honesty, there was nothing that could compare to how my emotions were fluctuating all over the place. Being angry or simply crying would, at least, provide some release for everything that kept coming to my mind. Let's be honest, how do you respond when the father of your child says that he thinks it's best for the child you share to go to Heaven? In other words, let him die.

As a mother, my heart broke into so many pieces that there were no words to really express the pain. The one thing I had to do was be quiet for a moment, even as the tears streamed down my face. My son deserved the opportunity to live, and there was no way that my heart could think otherwise. To keep from being consumed with anger, I cried for several hours. Then came the point that changed my life forever.

A thought came to mind. That thought said that I needed to have faith in God for my son's life. After having been raised in a Christian home, attending church, and being ordained as a pastor, I returned to the one thing that kept my sanity — my faith in God. Honestly, that was the only option for me to focus on. At the most challenging time in my life, prayer became the only solution. My ears couldn't listen to another person because my reaction would have been inappropriate if they said something off the wall. Crying out to God felt like the only thing I could do. It felt safe. Feeling as low, frustrated, hurt, and confused as I did, I only knew how to pray. Before I could open my mouth to pray, a fond memory came to mind, and it was when I preached a message about trusting God. My message was, no matter what you were faced with in life, just trust God.

After remembering this, I said to God, "I have heard Your Word all my life, and I have even preached Your Word to others; now, I will have to believe in it."

At this point, I knew about God being great, but it is here that I got to know God in a very personal and intimate manner. I'm going to be honest. It is easier to teach or preach about God to others; it is very difficult to have to apply that same Word to your own life. If I can be truly honest, I believed God's Word was for other people; I didn't believe it or in it for myself.

If you think for a moment and acknowledge that the reason you are in this moment is based on a decision you made, it is challenging to change the narrative that is happening in your own mind. Let's be truthful and genuine. We have all felt this way at some point in our Christian journey. I had to make some essential decisions about God and how He still loves me no matter what I've done.

Ironically, this was when I realized that I have studied God's Word all of these years, but I have never known Him. Wow! What a transformative moment for me when I realized that! The next few moments were critical to my faith walk with God from that day until now. I am not sure if I could ever go back to just knowing about God.

I said to God, "I am going to do what I have shared with others to do. Your Word is what I will stand on."

"I declared out of my own mouth that my son shall not die but live to declare the works of the Lord" (Psalm 118:17). I heard a very gentle voice say to me,

"Then, according to your faith, be it unto you" (Matthew 9:29, KJV). In other words, if you have the faith to believe in your son's life, then I will honor your faith.

At that very moment, I felt the pressure of everything that had just happened to me leave my body. If you have ever watched a movie and seen when someone left their body, but they could still look at themselves, that was what I felt happened to me. I knew that God had spoken directly to me, and I knew He felt my deep pain. And He didn't stop there. God proceeded to share with me that my life had just been transformed. Honestly, I didn't fully understand, but I knew that God was now in control. I had the confidence that, what I had just asked God to do, He was going to do it. It was amazing to experience a personal moment where the pain was devasting one minute, and the next moment, I heard God speak to me. Life can no longer go backward because I have to continue pursuing this newfound love and relationship with God. At that very moment, I realized how much God loved me and how He had always been there for me.

As I drifted off to sleep, I knew that I still had tears in my eyes, but the tears weren't from pain; they were tears of joy that came from the peace of knowing that God Himself was taking over this situation. Sleeping was the best medicine for the moment I was in. There are times when we have to stop and rest/sleep to allow our bodies to recover. I didn't just want my son to live; I wanted to live, too. When we are experiencing deep emotional pain, we have to be careful to not let that take us out of here.

A few hours into my sleep, I was awakened by Jeremiah's doctor. She briefly shared with me that the code blues he'd experienced were something she thought she knew would happened. The doctor was extraordinarily truthful and forthright about what she thought could have caused the code blues. She mentioned that she thought that Jeremiah had fluid on his heart. I asked, "What does that mean?"

She explained that too much fluid on a lung can stop a person's heart from beating. My inquisitive mind came to life, and I began to inquire about the options for Jeremiah. She shared that he would need surgery to remove the fluid. The surgery is called a pericardiocentesis. During our conversation, I asked, "Have you ever done this kind of surgery before?"

Her honest answer was "no." However, she proceeded to share with me that she believed she could do it.

Before I knew it, I asked her if there was another doctor within the area who had more experience doing this surgery. Her response was "yes." However, that doctor was located at another hospital. In order to get Jeremiah there, they would have had to care-flight him to that hospital. He was too critical and too small for them to move him. My next question was, What are we going to do? The doctor looked at me and shared that she had studied the procedure before speaking with me. I asked her with an in-your-face kind of look, "Do you think you can do the surgery?"

Her reply was, "Yes, I do."

I, then, said, "The only way I will allow you to do this surgery is if you allow my pastor to pray for you."

Her immediate response was "absolutely."

At that moment, the only thing that kept coming to mind was "there is power in prayer."

I picked up my phone, called my pastor, and shared with him what was happening. He, then, asked for me to put the doctor on the phone. He prayed over her, and I knew, at that moment, that God was with her. It was as if I heard God say to me, "Everything really is going to be all right." When the doctor left my room, she had tears in her eyes, as if she had heard God for herself.

A Life Lesson

When you're facing the scariest time in your life, pray or find someone else to pray for you. Don't rely on your own thoughts.

Chapter 2
Dependency on God

About four to six hours later, the doctor returned to my room. She said, "The next seventy-two hours are very critical." Additionally, she expressed, "The surgery went well, and we believe we got all of the fluid."

However, she was meticulous in what she described to me. Truthfully, her genuine concern for me was illustrated in how she handled me. There was peace in my room as I knew that God was on the scene.

Laying in that bed while my son was in surgery was so surreal. It felt like I was watching a movie on TV, but this was real life, and it was happening to me. What movie could I have been watching that would impact my emotions so significantly? Can you imagine the many thoughts I had in my head about how my one-pound-fifteen-ounces little boy could come through heart surgery? I was informed about what actually happened during surgery and how delicate the procedure was. The doctor disclosed that the surgery required two people and neither could make any sudden moves. It was so sensitive to movement that my son wouldn't be alive if one of them had made a sudden move. God had to have His hand on their hands for them to complete it. Let God teach you to trust and rely on Him when you don't know what else to do.

During those dreadful seventy-two hours, I tried to limit my conversation and who I talked to. One of the main reasons was I didn't want to hear anything that didn't make sense. I was not trying to be difficult, but people can say some of the craziest things during the most critical times. Truthfully, if someone came to me with too many words, I wasn't going to listen. I had to find a secret place to hide my heart and mind. I discovered the best place for me was depending on God in the quietness and being patient.

Of course, my nurses had to do their jobs and get me back up on my feet by getting me out of bed. I had to get out of bed and go for walks. They thought it was a good idea that I walk down to the NICU and see Jeremiah. God was always on the scene because, each time I went to the NICU, other parents were there, and they were in a situation similar to mine. Not one of the parents knew anything, and all of us were praying for our children. The one common theme was that we didn't care about anything else other than the health of our children. There was no discussion centered around whether we were all Christians, what church we went to, or our nationalities. The common denominator was our children, who were in need of critical care.

The parents all knew that Jeremiah had had surgery, and they rallied around me to ensure I had support. It was like I had a new family that immediately responded to my need to not be alone.

As I approached Jeremiah's incubator, he was still in a critical place, and the machines were going off. My heart kept sinking, but I came to grips with the fact that I had to depend on God to get through these moments. The support of the other parents really helped me not to break down. If my emotions had had their way, they would have put me in a strait jacket, and I would have been hugging myself. However, I didn't let them go wild.

A Resting Place

For the next three days, my faith had to kick in so strong that I couldn't allow one thing to get me off-course. I learned that God's love for me was genuine and experiential. Our God is always with us, even when we are in extremely difficult places in life. I knew, without a shadow of a doubt in my mind, that God loved Jeremiah and me. I may not have known what was going to happen next, but I had an assurance that Jeremiah was going to pull through. There are times when your only reliance is on the dependency of God.

Every night, as I slept, there was an exceptional peace that came over me. I didn't need any pain pills or any sleeping medication. The nurses who cared for me were surprised to see how peaceful I was during this critical time. The funny thing was I had to take a look at myself and say, "Are you all right?"

It was funny to me because I didn't panic or allow fear to rule. Did scary thoughts enter my mind? Yes, they did, and I had to immediately change those thoughts because the reality was my medically-fragile child, who wasn't even two pounds, was recovering from a surgery that drained fluid from his heart.

The three days passed, and Jeremiah woke up and responded to the oxygen and the touches from the medical staff. Whenever the doctors described the look on the medical team's faces, it was a sense of relief. Jeremiah wasn't out of the woods completely, but he had made it through the critical seventy-two hours. I thought back to that moment when the doctor said that he was out of crucial surgery mode. I had tears, but this time, they were from the joy of knowing that God was in the midst of everything. There were many tough days ahead of me, but now my faith had increased to believe that Jeremiah's life would continue.

It was my last night at the hospital. They planned to discharge me the following day. Before going to sleep, I asked God to extend my time at the hospital. Discovering a resting place in God allowed me to pray, and I watched God move. Early in the morning, the nurse entered my room to tell me when I would be discharged. I requested to speak to the charge nurse. I told the nurse that it wasn't to complain but to ask a question.

When the charge nurse arrived, I simply asked her if I could stay at the hospital. She was fully aware of what was happening with my son, so she left the room to go to the administration on my behalf. After she left, I had this peace that came and sat on me, letting me know that she would be coming back with a favorable response. Having faith in God and belief can, indeed, change your life. She entered my room with a definite answer of "yes." The nurse explained that they had rooms for parents whose children had had surgery that I could stay in. I moved to the new room and then went to the NICU.

Relying on God...Brings about Results

All of the nurses in the NICU got to know me well, as I spent lots of time with each one of them while taking care of Jeremiah. During our many discussions, I learned the reason why each of them chose to work in the NICU. It was great to hear their backgrounds and to hear how many of them loved their job. This comforted me because I wasn't sure how long Jeremiah would be in the NICU. In time, I found out that many of them were Christians and believed in the power of prayer.

Interestingly, even if they weren't Christians or believed in something else, they all agreed that prayer was powerful. A fleeting thought entered my mind, If they all believed in prayer, why not ask them to join me in prayer? Many of them never had a problem with me wanting to pray. The hearts and compassion of these nurses were definitely a direct reflection of God's very presence.

Our prayer time included other families, as they all needed something miraculous to happen for their child or children. Being in this place with so much uncertainty around me, believing in something bigger than me was critical. I wasn't smart enough to know how to walk through this time in my life alone. I had to reach deep down within myself and find the one thing that gave me strength, and that was my Lord and Savior, Jesus Christ. Yes, being a believer was the best thing for me because I don't know how I could have made it.

We had twenty-four-hour access to visit our children in the NICU, and this was a good and bad thing. I wanted to be up there every minute of the day, and it took one of the nurses to shed some light on an essential factor — I needed to get some rest. The extra days I had in the hospital were great because I could go downstairs to my room and rest. It was easy to be at the hospital.

Boy, things changed when I had to go home. Everything inside of me felt the pain of the situation all over again. The only thought that wondered in my mind was, I'm going to be too far away from Jeremiah. You would think I lived hours away. I was less than twenty minutes away from the hospital, but those twenty minutes seemed like a three-day-long trip across the country. I know that sounds extreme, but that is what I felt each time I went home.

As a mother, I felt helpless and like I was abandoning my child. The guilty feeling overtook my thoughts and almost sent me in a downward spiral of depression. There were many days I didn't know if I was coming or going. Lord knows I didn't know what was happening with Jeremiah. Many days, it looked as if nothing was improving, and sometimes, it was worse because there were declines.

There was one dreadful time when the nurses met me in the hallway before I entered the NICU. My heart sank, and all I could think was Jeremiah was no longer here. Tears and fear gripped my very soul. They pulled me aside and sat me down. I asked them, "What happened?"

They wanted to prepare me for what I was going to see when I went to Jeremiah's incubator. This moment was confusing and emotionally too much for me to even fathom. The team of nurses shared that needles were coming out of his brain, and that could scare someone if they had never seen that before. I looked at them as if they were speaking a foreign language. I asked, "Why?"

They explained that the peripherally inserted central catheter (PICC) lines they had in his legs and feet were no longer working. Of course, I had no idea what a PICC line was, so everything was too much for my brain to absorb, but after the nurses took the time to explain, I then proceeded to go to the NICU.

Whoosh! Honestly, I cried and cried some more. Seeing my little son with more needles in his tiny body than I had ever seen on another person before in my entire life was difficult. He looked so fragile and almost lifeless. The tears were coming down my face profusely. The nurses assured me that he was doing well and getting what he needed. When they spoke to me, sometimes the words went through one ear and out the other. However, when I calmed down and regained my composure, I heard a quiet, still voice. It said, "He's going to be all right. Just trust Me with his life."

At that moment, I experienced the sweetest feeling all over my body that sent chills up my spine. It was so different, but it felt amazingly good. My tears dried up, and I could share with the others and the nurses. When I told them what happened, you could have heard a pin drop in the NICU. Moments like that happened a few times during Jeremiah's stay in the NICU. I put all of my trust in God and found an ounce of strength to believe. The journey was nowhere near over, but I learned how to embrace those times when God showed up.

A Life Lesson

When you no longer have the strength and you feel hopeless, you must understand that God is with you and will give you strength for each moment.

Chapter 3

Hearing God in the Midst of Many Voices

Experiencing a crisis in the Neonatal Intensive Care Unit is an experience that is, honestly, hard to describe. It is one of the most critical and hopeful environments. You have babies fighting for their lives while families are weeping and feeling deep despair. The hope comes in when you listen to the nurses who share stories about the tiny babies that grow up to be healthy and live long lives. They've witnessed the worst of times and the best of times. Not every story ends well, but many of them do because of the great medicine and technology that are available. Who would think that my son, being one pound and fifteen ounces, would ever grow up?

The following eighty-plus days were spent listening to many voices speak about what was happening with Jeremiah. I heard everything from "we may need to insert a G-tube in him to feed him and help him grow" to "a tracheotomy will give him the ability to breathe." They said that, due to a lack of oxygen, he had experienced some brain bleeds or hemorrhaging.

The words that were used took me to a dark place mainly because I didn't understand anything that was being said or how it was impacting Jeremiah.

My weakest subject in school was science. I did just enough to get a passing grade, and the rest was left to the mercy of God to see me through. I cringed when medical terms were spoken to me, and I had to literally ask millions of questions just to understand what anyone was saying about Jeremiah's condition. I had to face some hard truths during this time, but that allowed me to realize that all of the voices were speaking in a language that was way out of my comfort zone. The great thing about this time, though, was nobody ever made me feel inadequate. They were so good that they would give me material to read, so I could make better decisions. I took those pamphlets home and reviewed them. I also used the internet to research everything they shared before deciding on the next steps.

The hospital took things one step further and connected me with other parents who had gone through a similar journey. I was able to speak with them and learn how they got through it. Conversing with others who could relate helped me not to be afraid about making a decision. However, after all of the research and conversation, I had to stop and pray. There were too many voices in my head. I had to seek God and ask for His wisdom. Ironically, not having a solid medical background provided a better doorway for God to share His wisdom. This is to say, I could do nothing but rely on God's wisdom.

The questions came back around when I discussed the essential milestones that Jeremiah needed to reach while in the NICU. It was clearly explained that he had to gain weight before he could go home. Despite the other medical fragilities he was experiencing, the weight gain was an essential component. My series of questions about all of the options presented to me created a long conversation. I could only imagine that, deep down, these doctors and nurses wanted me to stop asking all these questions. Here I was, in my position as his mother, not fully understanding the impact of each recommendation.

When they wanted to put a tracheotomy in his throat, my question was simple, Is this a life-or-death situation? I wanted to know if this was something that was being done out of convenience to speed up the process or something that was required for him. They proceeded to share that it would help him, but the oxygen tube connected to him was helping him to breathe. My mommy's mind came front and center because a trachea would require me to keep it clean. One thing about me, and I must be very transparent. I have a weak stomach. Would I have implemented the tracheotomy if it was life or death? Absolutely! It was something that I would have done and done it afraid. Mothers step up to the plate and do whatever we have to for our children to live. It was the wisdom of the Lord that prompted me to ask them if it was a life-or-death situation. It gave me a better way to respond to the request. "If the connected oxygen provided adequate support," I said, "let's wait and see how Jeremiah improves."

The key was I didn't have peace about them cutting a hole in my son's neck that would have to be maintained when he got home.

Once again, we gathered together as Jeremiah's team and discussed the insertion of a G-tube. Imagine with me, for a moment, as I sat there with all these wonderful doctors and nurses. I was trying to decide which one was about to move in with me. They really didn't understand me because I would ensure Jeremiah was good, but I would have stopped eating. So eventually, the weight concern wouldn't have been about Jeremiah; it would have been about me. I said to God, with the most sincere heart, "Lord, you know me and my stomach. Lord, you know how much I can handle, and this right here would take me to another level."

I had a laugh within myself because God knew what I was dealing with. The wisdom of God is better than anything I could have learned. Here we were again, and I asked the question, "Is the G-tube a life-or-death situation for him?"

They all came back with different perspectives, and I wondered if we could wait for a few more weeks. If it was a life-or-death decision, then let's do it. Given that the team of doctors and nurses had learned a lot about me, they knew I wasn't going to agree if it wasn't required.

After several meetings, we decided that they would keep the feeding tube running through his nose as the source of his nutrients. We stated that we would introduce feeding Jeremiah through a bottle once he gained a few more pounds. I can't describe how much relief I experienced after we decided to give him some more time to grow. I know God was speaking to me in the midst of all of my nerves going every which way they wanted. One thing I've learned is God will give you His wisdom if you ask for it.

Different Way of Doing Things

As time went by and a few weeks had passed, Jeremiah began to grow. He was still connected to all the machines and needed oxygen to breathe, but there was some progress. He grew to three and half pounds, and it was time to see if he would take a bottle.

Here is an interesting thing that happens whenever you have a premature baby. As a mother, you don't get to hold your child right away. It depends on the condition of the child as to when you will get to hold him. I had to wait for a couple of weeks. During this time, I could only look at Jeremiah and touch his tiny fingers through a hole in the incubator.

Full disclosure: I felt like less than a mother because I couldn't even feed or change my child's diaper. These are things that we are expected to do from day one. I felt I had been robbed of the very thing that I was supposed to do, and it was a humiliating feeling. Things were out of my control, but I was ready to nurture and care for my child. I had waited until I was in my early forties, and then I couldn't even perform the tasks I was created to do. Those days of feeling like I was on an emotional roller coaster were real and very prevalent in my life.

However, I would pull myself together with the help of the Lord each time I visited Jeremiah. The one thing that I was reminded of by other parents who had gone through or were going through this was that the energy you give to your child has to remain positive. Even in an incubator, Jeremiah could feel my power.

There were many times when I had to step away from him to gather my composure. This wasn't an easy thing to do at times. Other times, it was easy because, somehow, Jeremiah would smile when he heard my voice. He knew when I was there and would respond. It gave me a source of strength and the fortitude to keep going. There is never a right or wrong way to process this kind of experience.

I would go to the NICU two to three times a

day. I would call every two hours until the nurses knew, when the phone rang at certain times, that it was me. They would answer that Jeremiah was doing well and that he was resting. Then, they would say, "Go to bed" with a smile.

Once it was safe for Jeremiah to be out of the incubator for a while, they taught me how to hold him while preparing to feed him. The way they taught me to hold him was called *kangarooing*. This is a process where they placed my baby directly on my skin. I held him for about one hour. Let me say, the first time I held my son, the feeling of joy that consumed my mind and body was overwhelming. It was a positive feeling. He was so tiny, but he felt so good against my skin. At that very moment, I felt like a mother. This came after weeks of waiting, so much had hindered this process. But not with Jeremiah and me. He knew me, and I knew him.

The nurses had made this little orange hat for him that was small enough to fit a baby doll's head. This orange hat covered his tiny head as they slipped him under my shirt, and I just sat there. No one said much to me because they could see tears of joy flowing down my face. A nurse sat with me to ensure that I didn't get scared. He still had a lot of tubes, needles, and other medical equipment attached to him. I had to be right next to the incubator.

Figure 1. Mommy holding JD for the first time.

While we were sitting in the rocking chair, Jeremiah fell asleep. When my hour was up, and they saw how peaceful he was, they allowed us another hour. I was so thankful for God's favor on my life. In these times, I learned the value of life and how important it is to love unconditionally. Jeremiah was the cutest tiny little baby I had ever seen. Keep in mind that's not just because he was my son, but he had started to fill out and look good. Subsequently, when Jeremiah reached four pounds, he was ready to eat from a bottle. Furthermore, we had learned each other during the times I held him until I believed he was ready to try something with a little more sustenance. There was a feeding therapist that met me at Jeremiah's bed/incubator. Interestingly, he grew out of his closed incubator into one that had an opening. Yes, I could now help with changing his diaper. What a great feeling that was the first time I changed him. I cried, but they were joyful tears because I was caring for my son.

When I got the handle of feeding him through a bottle, it was on and poppin'. I was a mom who was ready to nurture my son. The feeling I was looking for became my reality, and I was immeasurably joyful. Jeremiah learned how to get his food from the bottle. Eventually, the feeding tube in his nose was removed. He was gaining weight, and things were looking up for him.

Our approach was to let Jeremiah be the one to tell us when he was ready to make a change. I didn't understand the medical aspect, but my mother instincts kicked into gear. I refused to believe that we had to do anything physically to his body in order for him to grow.

Some doctors probably didn't like that I wasn't eager to infringe upon Jeremiah by cutting him. This little boy had already experienced heart surgery on the first day of his life. I didn't want to add any more trauma to his little body. I respected the doctors, but I had to have them respect me as his mother. I never hesitated to share with them that I was doing this based on my faith in God. Yes, I was bold and very courageous about my relationship with God. I didn't have anything else that I believed in more than I believed in God.

As the days continued, Jeremiah grew, and some of the needles were removed from his feet and head. He started to look like my little baby boy. He had grown to over four and a half pounds. We were a few pounds away from being discharged. His health became stable enough that the only tube he had was his oxygen. He had other monitors but no more needles, of course, unless they were taking his blood. His complexion was

shining, and his smile was radiant. I was a proud mother who was so grateful to God for His grace in Jeremiah's life.

A Life Lesson

Asking questions and gleaning wisdom from God will give you peace of mind. Even when you don't fully understand, God will teach you what to do. Don't ever be afraid to ask a question.

Chapter 4
My Child is Blessed, Not Cursed

Here we are, still in the NICU, and while witnessing all of Jeremiah's transformations, I had to wonder why this happened. There was a fleeting thought, My child came into this world as a result of my disobedience to God. Not being married and preaching the gospel, I would be remiss if I said that thought never crossed my mind. There were others who had thought the same thing and expressed that to me, as well.

Initially, when I heard it, I was deeply wounded. Then, I heard God clearly say, "I don't need to hurt you." He told me that my son is a blessing to me. As a matter of fact, He shared that my son would be a blessing to many others. He was very adamant that Jeremiah's life would bring hope to others.

What made this whole thing oxymoronic was that God's mercy and grace were the only things that kept Jeremiah and me going. I had to silence people and my own thoughts. We have to be honest with God and ourselves. It is what brought a change in my life. I learned very quickly that children are a blessing from the Lord, not a curse. I rejected the religious theories and thought processes of others and acknowledged the unconditional love of God.

I am so glad that I learned this early on in Jeremiah's life. I started seeing him as a huge blessing, even though I had no idea what the coming days would be like. All I knew was that this little boy was a miracle who had already defied the minds of his doctors and nurses.

My light for Jesus shined even when I was crying. It is was important that I be truthful to God as to where I was each moment. When I wasn't my best self, I would allow God to cover me with His grace. Strangely enough, no one ever said to me, "We thought you lost your faith."

It was the complete opposite of what was communicated to me. The nurses and other parents felt the strength of God coming from my life. Did I understand everything that was happening to Jeremiah? Absolutely not at all. The only assurance I had was that I always believed that God was with me during every tear, step, and dramatic moment.

The blessing of a child can improve your outlook

on life and change the very trajectory of how you approach life. Before Jeremiah came along, I was searching for unconditional love, and all this time, I had the best lover of all. I never fully understood the love of God until Jeremiah was born.

When I became a mother, I immediately forgot about everything concerning myself, and right away, life had new meaning. Another life was dependent on me, and I had to give of myself without hesitation. It didn't matter what Jeremiah needed; I was willing to learn, do, and advocate for him. We, sometimes, call it being a "Mama Bear" when it comes to our children. What a blessing to die to yourself for the sake of someone else.

My focus was on loving Jeremiah and letting him know that I believed in him, no matter what he was facing. This sounds so similar to what Christ did when He laid down His life for us. He didn't focus on His thoughts, His feelings, or, even, His needs. All He wanted was to give us the opportunity to be reconciled with God. He was focused on His purpose.

Living a Life without Understanding the Environment

Jeremiah was growing in the NICU, and there weren't many days left before he would be coming home. Many questions became prominent to me because coming home meant something different than the original plan. What was the home environment going to look like? Would I have to take any of this medical equipment home? Would I even know what to do when I got home? The laundry list of questions plagued my mind daily.

One of the most incredible things they had in place was required training for the parents before taking a child home. This was a relief for me because I would be able to ask all of my questions while learning. Due to the number of different types of medical equipment that had to come home with my son, I got to stay two nights and learn how to take care of him.

On the first night, they brought Jeremiah into the room. They proceed to say, "He's all yours."

And the panicked look on my face let them know that I needed a little more assistance. They taught me how to feed, burp, and change him with all of the equipment attached. He required oxygen, so there were all of these oxygen tanks sitting next to the bed. Another fleeting thought came to mind, Where is all of this stuff going to fit? I had to take everything upstairs to my apartment. Yes, there were stairs, and all of this equipment would have to be carried up those stairs.

The first night, we were able to settle in, and then, it was feeding time. It went good, but the burping was challenging because of all the equipment attached. The nurses taught me some better ways to do things once I got home. They revealed that my mother's instinct would kick in, and I wouldn't be nervous. It was the hospital environment that brought about more stress, they said. I had never recognized how a hospital environment impacted my thinking.

The first night went well. I spoke with my son's many doctors, and they went over all the rules for the home. They highlighted that there should be no smoking and not to panic if the machines kept going off. They shared with me the critical things to look for and how to respond. My nerves were very much alive, but I still had time to get my questions answered.

On the second night of training, I had to give him a bath. Imagine with me a little over-five-pound little boy having to get a bath. I learned how to remove the different monitors. It was okay for him to not have oxygen for a few minutes. Jeremiah's health had improved so much that he could be without it for about two to three minutes. That was progress; however, it made me extremely nervous because I didn't want him to stop breathing.

Amid a significant life challenge, God will teach us some things about Himself. I became aware that every breath we breathe is from God. Here I was, afraid of Jeremiah not being on the oxygen; meanwhile, God reminded me that it's His breath that we breathe anyway. Who would have thought of the many things God wants us to learn in the middle of a trying time? The rest of the night went exceptionally well.

Everyone felt as if I was ready to take Jeremiah home. To be honest, I was afraid, but they didn't know that. During this time, there were numerous challenging thoughts running through my mind. The thoughts that ran throughout my mind, only God would understand. I had to own up to the fact that Jeremiah would heal better at home. It wasn't Jeremiah that I was concerned about; however, it was whether I could take care of him. What would I do if something happened? The real question was, How was I going to handle all of this alone?

My home was our new place, and I needed to keep the atmosphere peaceful. I may not have understood how things would play out at home, but I knew I needed to create a nurturing and healing environment. The first thing I did was find some Christian worship music. I had it playing twenty-four hours a day. This was similar to what I did when Jeremiah was in the NICU, when he was moved to a private room. In this room, he had a roommate, and the two of them, somehow, connected. Strangely, they knew when the other was in the room.

When his roommate's parents visited, I told them that Jeremiah would make sounds every time their son made sounds. Their medical equipment would beep almost at the same time. It was as if they wanted us to know "we got this, and we're going to be all right."

Fascinatingly, Jeremiah's roommate, at that time, was a little boy as well. His parents were youth pastors at their church. They didn't mind having worship music playing in our children's room. Whenever either one of us was visiting, we would each read scriptures to our children. Isn't it like God to place you with the right people at the right time?

This remarkable couple didn't know that I was very grateful that they included my son in their prayers, worship, and reading of the Word. I took so much comfort in knowing that, even in tribulation, God allowed our paths to cross.

Interestingly, even at this present time, our children are still connected. They never forgot about Jeremiah or me. We spent their first birthdays together. It was an honor to see how amazing God is and works in our lives.

So once my son was released from the hospital, my home became a place of worship, and Jeremiah loved it. I could tell right away that he loved music. He would respond with a smile when he heard it. Of course, there were plenty of other sounds happening at home that included the medical equipment. I had a pulse ox monitor, sleep monitor, oxygen tube, and a long list of daily medications.

A mother wears many different hats. One of the many hats I wore included "Nurse Jacquie." I monitored his oxygen level, made sure it hadn't desaturated. I made sure he wasn't having trouble breathing. While he was sleeping, I monitored him to make sure he didn't stopped breathing altogether. I gave him his medications using various methods and had to ensure it was the correct amount. Taking care of my son's medical needs was my first priority.

Additionally, keeping a peaceful home was my second priority. This resulted in me living alone until I could get some help. There were many sleepless nights for me, but knowing that Jeremiah was still alive and growing was enough to keep me going.

A Life Lesson

There are times when you have to do things that make you uncomfortable. However, it is in those times that you grow in faith and strength. You never know what you can handle until you are faced with adversity. Then, you get to experience God in a whole new way.

Chapter 5
What I Know for Sure

The lonely days and nights all seemed to run together. I didn't know what day of the week it was, and I certainly didn't sleep or eat well. Jeremiah's medical condition should have immediately qualified him for nursing assistance. Honestly, I didn't even understand what that meant because I had never seen anything like this before. Before nursing even came up for discussion, Jeremiah started receiving Early Childhood Intervention (ECI) services. This is where I learned what I needed and what I could receive to help me in the home. All I knew was that I could not keep having sleepless nights and not eating. It was hard to even get to a grocery store. I only had a few people I could call to assist me with just getting some of the basic items I needed.

The first time I left our home was to take Jeremiah to one of his pediatrician's appointments. Can I tell you that it was one of the scariest things ever! I had to carry oxygen tanks with us. I had to disconnect the monitors and hope that nothing happened. Then, I had to place him in the rear-facing car seat. I would be driving a good thirty minutes, and I would not be able to see him in his car seat. You talk about being nervous. That was an understatement for me during that time.

When we made it to his first appointment, the staff could see the fatigue on my face. They could see I was so stressed out. When we got to see the nurse practitioner, she did everything she could think of to calm me down. I must have looked like a complete hot mess. Truthfully, I didn't even know what I looked like, nor did I care. I was grateful to have made it there in one piece. I love to drive, but that thirty-minute ride caused more neck and shoulder pain from the tension I felt than a full-day, cross-country drive.

They checked Jeremiah out and shared that he was doing well. I had to take him back to the doctor in thirty days. In the meantime, there were other medical specialists that they wanted Jeremiah to see. The laundry list of doctors was overwhelming, but they helped get all of the contact information together.

I now was wearing the hat of being Jeremiah's administrative assistant. We left the doctor's office with marching orders in hand and a long thirty-minute drive ahead. Making it back home safely was the goal, and we did just that. It was connecting him back to all the monitors that was nerve-wracking. Feeding him, changing his diapers, and keeping him calm were what I focused on and spent most of my time doing.

The one crucial component for me was that I knew that my son was going to live. I didn't know what would be needed, but I was sure he had a purpose in life. When I saw God continuously answering a prayer that had been prayed the very first day of his life, that kept my faith growing and hope in the air. I may not have known what he would experience or even need, but I know that God created him. That's what I leaned on when I became weak. In a given twenty-four-hour period, I would be high on faith and then lower than a hopeless person. It was a massive undertaking that hit my life drastically that I couldn't explain to anyone. The one true thing would be my need for help in the coming days, months, and years.

Home Life Needed a Makeover

One night, while I was attempting to sleep, the monitors wouldn't stop for anything. It seemed, as soon as my eyelids closed, they would go off again. I cried out to God, "Lord, I need some help!"

The following day, my goddaughter Iesha (who I call "my daughter") called to check on us. I shared with her that, although Jeremiah was doing good, I hadn't slept in weeks. The concern in her voice was very evident. As she proceeded to tell me how her online classes were going, a light bulb went off in my head. You could say God revealed to me that I could ask her to come and stay with me for a few months. When it was my turn to talk again, I asked her that very question. She immediately responded with an enthusiastic "yes." I told her that I needed to speak with her mother first.

Later that night, I spoke with her mom, and she agreed. Within five days, Iesha had moved into my home. What a relief it was just having another adult in the house. Honestly, she was an answer to my prayers. I shared with her all that Jeremiah had going on and what we needed to do to take care of him. She was so excited to be able to give me a chance to sleep. We created a weekly schedule of who was on-duty on which days. We had to sleep and eat right whenever we were off-duty. Sharing the load helped me think clearer and learn more about Jeremiah's needs.

After a few weeks, we had a working schedule that supported Jeremiah's and our needs. He was growing and eating more. We had a therapy schedule that worked, and he was on his way to developing the necessary skills. Due to the brain damage he experienced at birth, he needed a lot of assistance. I made all of his appointments with the other medical specialists. We went to see about five additional doctors. Each one of them specialized in an area that Jeremiah was challenged in. We saw a neurologist, pulmonologist, gastroenterologist, and an ophthalmologist, to name a few.

Here comes Nurse Jacquie, back on the scene, as I met with each of them. Learning about the body requires you to know how to ask a lot of questions. Each doctor gave the care instructions we should follow while he was at home. We adhered to them all, and Jeremiah continued to grow stronger.

A Moment of Disbelief

One day, my daughter and I decided to play a game to relax our minds. While we were playing,

Jeremiah was lying in his crib. At one point, my daughter got up to go to the bathroom. As she did so, she happened to look over at Jeremiah and saw that he was turning blue. She said, "Mom, call 911! Jeremiah is turning blue and not breathing!"

I picked up my phone in a sheer panic and called 911, while my daughter did CPR on Jeremiah. The 911 operator asked me to explain precisely what was happening and let me know that EMS was on its way. I was so scared that I couldn't be still long enough to help my daughter. I even ran around the house and went into the closet looking for my socks. Yes, my nerves got the best of me at that very moment. Thankfully, my daughter was doing exactly what the 911 operator said to do. It only took one of us to resuscitate Jeremiah until he started breathing again. We were able to increase his oxygen levels before EMS arrived. By the time they reached my home, Jeremiah was just fine.

Jeremiah experienced turning blue one other time, and we went through the same process. The next time he stopped breathing and turned blue, I was in a much better space because I had been through this scenario before. When the medical team arrived,

Jeremiah was laughing and playing. You would think that he had not ever stopped breathing.

As time passed, Jeremiah would continue to get stronger. Finally, the time came where he decided to remove the oxygen tube from his nose. Immediately, I would replace it.

One night, Iesha and I woke up in the middle of the night and discovered that he had taken his oxygen tube out of his nose again and was sleeping with no oxygen on. We went back and forth for several days. I even got creative and used medical tape to secure the tubing in his nose.

His personality was starting to shine through, and he demonstrated a stubbornness that let me know that he was going to do what he wanted to do. He was so determined that the oxygen tube was not going to remain in his nose. He would wait until we were asleep to remove it.

Keep in mind, Jeremiah had stopped breathing in my care at home a couple of times. I quickly learned that he was sending us a message that he knew he could breathe without it. Indeed, that is exactly what he was communicating to us.

The Assurance of Life

The stubbornness Jeremiah showed helped me, as his mother. It let me know that he was determined to live. After several weeks of him removing his oxygen, Jeremiah, my daughter, and I went to see his pulmonologist. During our visit, I told her about how he had repeatedly removed his oxygen tube. After hearing this, Jeremiah's pulmonologist agreed to remove the oxygen. But only after she asked us, "Did his oxygen level desaturate at any time?"

My daughter and I both enthusiastically answered, "No!"

Jeremiah was sure that he wanted to live without anything up his nose. The great thing that came out of it was we had two less machines to contend with, and he could sleep freely. Jeremiah's thrust for life gave me an assurance that he was determined to fight for his life. We eventually got rid of the oxygen tanks. We didn't have to use the pulse ox machine, only to check his saturation levels at different times during the day. Please understand that we were happy to see it go because it was the loudest machine at night.

Jeremiah's inspiration for wanting to live continued in how he fought to have those things removed from his nose. He was growing and improving. Even when he overcame the need for supplemental oxygen, there was still a lot going on with him. As a result of the brain damage, there were some severe cognitive delays and physical impairments. It was difficult for him to hold up his own head for several months. He wasn't able to sit up, so the therapist would continue to work with him.

The one key thing I kept seeing in Jeremiah was determination. It kept me hoping that anything could change in his life, if I could only believe. The worship music was still being played in our home, and daily prayer always happened. My pastor would pray with me and for Jeremiah often. It was a blessing to have so many others praying for Jeremiah. When things became more challenging and Jeremiah had to go back into the hospital, it was the strength of the prayers of others that helped me keep my sanity.

There were many questions about what Jeremiah's future would look like. There was no doctor or medical professional that could give a definitive answer to that question. Their focus was on the day-to-day obstacles that we had to work through. In some cases, we overcame them, and in other cases, it required a different way of living. I was grateful for everything that positively happened in Jeremiah's life. This provoked a fleeting thought within me. Why is his life so significant? I wondered. Why was I so committed to doing or learning how to nurture him? Of course, this was not what I thought my life would be like, but Jeremiah's life was worth it.

A Life Lesson

It may become extremely difficult to understand the challenges you are facing, but always know your why or reason for doing what you do. In the process, you will grow in faith and in the belief that things will get better. Keep moving forward and don't focus on the challenges. Focus on the victories, no matter their size.

Chapter 6
Laugh, Pray, Live

As the months continued to pass, all I did was take care of Jeremiah's medical needs. I didn't know how to laugh anymore, nor did I believe I should be laughing because of what was happening in my life. My focus was on keeping Jeremiah alive and constantly learning about what was happening to him. The stress of everything started to really get to me. There were days I didn't know what to do or not to do, especially when it seemed like things were not progressing, but things were progressing, just not at the pace I wanted. Jeremiah was growing, but there was minimal movement with his body. He didn't know what challenges he was facing, but I knew he wasn't developing at a child's pace at his current age.

Jeremiah was my first child, and I really didn't know what to expect from his development. The only thing I had were my family members asking me if Jeremiah was crawling or holding his head up. Silly me, I was responding, "No, not at this time." I didn't fully grasp what they were asking me or why. All I knew was Jeremiah was breathing on his own, and I was happy about that.

As time went by, I researched the various milestones for child development and realized that Jeremiah was falling behind. My mother instinct kicked in, and my mind started wondering, What am I going to do? Candidly, I began to panic and thought, What if? And the list of questions began. My daughter stopped me dead in my tracks and asked me whose report would I believe. Wow! That was a slap in my face, but one that was needed at that very moment. It was, during times like this, when things gripped my heart. That was when God would show up for me and remind me that He was still in control.

I needed to be reassured that, whatever was happening with Jeremiah daily, was not something I could have stopped, prevented, or even made worse. The one critical thing was that I found a way to stop for a moment and breathe. I never knew how vital stopping for myself would be, especially in terms of how it impacted Jeremiah.

One day, in a very transparent moment, I told

my daughter that I was tired and that I couldn't keep going at this rate. I needed to get a better perspective on things to be more effective in my decision-making on Jeremiah's behalf. When she heard me say that, there was an immediate agreement. I realized that I had stopped doing the things that helped me to cope with life. Truthfully, I had stopped living and had almost forgotten about how important I was. This is so easy to do when you are caring for someone else. Self-care gets removed when your child is totally dependent on you. In reality, my and Jeremiah's lives were truly dependent on God and His wisdom and strength. With minimal progression in Jeremiah's physical body, it became apparent that he would need 100 percent daily assistance.

A Quest to Laugh

There were so many times when I would look at Jeremiah's face, and no matter what he had been through, he would be smiling. I found that he was ticklish, and that became the way I played with him. Then, it hit me one day — if he could smile every day, there's got to be something for me to smile about. I said within myself, "I have to find a way to laugh again. My life is not over, and I have to rediscover it."

I made a conscious decision to find something that I enjoyed doing, something that made me laugh, and do it. Prior to Jeremiah's birth, I would watch a good comedy and laugh throughout the film. So, I searched for the latest comedy that was in theaters and went to see it. I left the house because I needed to embrace the whole experience of going to a movie. That did me so much good. Doing something for me, something that made me laugh, was so important. When I started laughing again, my perspective on my situation changed as well. I began to see things with the hope that what was happening would get better. I had to believe that, no matter what I was seeing.

It's Prayer Time

My belief and hope that things would get better became the transition I needed to help Jeremiah and myself. Before I had remembered to laugh, I had forgotten, for a moment, that prayer is a powerful tool to have. Prayer allowed me to express to God how I was really feeling. My prayer time was therapeutic. It helped me to maintain my sanity, and it kept peace in the home. It was essential for Jeremiah because, during that time, when God spoke to me, He told me about who Jeremiah was created to be.

I have learned that prayer is a two-way communication between us and God. Prayer is a time for us to share and a time for us to listen. I had so much to share that I had to be still long enough to listen.

When we are hurting, we want someone to listen to our pain. However, I learned that I really needed to listen to God so that I could learn how to live again. Boy, at that time, there was such a heavy emphasis on Jeremiah's medical needs that it was the only topic of conversation for a while. Then, reality hit me. I realized that Jeremiah needed to learn that there was more to life than a medical condition. I had to begin to live while still caring for him because it was good for him to see me doing daily tasks and things that I enjoyed like cooking or watching a television show. As he began to see that I enjoyed things, he became open to exploring toys and other forms of entertainment.

God often shares insight on how we can change our situations, but we can miss it, especially if we think it has to come in a particular package. No matter how challenging things may have gotten, I had to believe that my life was not over and God had a plan for my life. It was during prayer that I learned more about what was happening with Jeremiah medically. The Lord would share a topic for me to research, and my eyes would be so enlightened by the information I'd just read. Our God will get us to the point where He knows we will listen. I had to stop focusing only on Jeremiah and start focusing on me. That wasn't easy, but with prayer, I was able to start living again. Living was different, but it was something I believed God had in store for me.

My daughter and I started taking days "off," and during this time, we would do whatever we wanted. We had nurses in the home caring for Jeremiah, so we knew he was good. With this knowledge, we started having fun and living again. It felt strange at first because we had become so accustomed to constantly caring for Jeremiah and always being on call. It was now time to pick up the new hat called "I am Living Again." This was something that became very important. We even started teaching that to Jeremiah.

Once Jeremiah had gotten a little older, around

the age of three years old, we started taking him to different parks and putting him on swings. The smiles on his face during each new experience were priceless. He loved to swing and didn't mind going high at all. Although he wasn't able to speak at this time, his facial expressions communicated a whole lot to me.

One of the daily habits that I started doing was taking a few hours a day and committing it to God in prayer, reading my Word, and worshipping. I felt a need to keep the right atmosphere in the home in order to bring about emotional, physical, and spiritual healing. The more consistent I was, the more God would teach me that His ways were not our ways. This meant that things would happen in His timing. I couldn't rush anything, no matter how much I wanted something to happen. I kept praying about Jeremiah's health and his ability to speak. I prayed for God to lead me in another important decision. I needed God's help in deciding whether to put my son in public school or private school after he turned three. We had to do this because he would no longer be eligible to receive the ECI services.

Life Adventures

When Jeremiah was still very young, we didn't allow that to stop us from going around other people. That was a challenge at first because many people didn't know what to say when they first saw Jeremiah. It was always awkward when people would meet Jeremiah and notice that he had leg braces and was in a wheelchair. Often, he would be rocking back and forth. But other people's reactions didn't stop us, though. We continued to meet up with our friends and venture out. We went to sporting events, zoos, museums, and other great places to have fun. We even took public transportation, so he would know what that experience was like. It is my firm belief that exposure is one critical factor for raising a child who's been diagnosed with a disability. If you think about it, exposure is good for all children.

My focus had to change in order for both Jeremiah and I to live. Don't get me wrong. Jeremiah's medical issues were still front and center, but he needed to see that he could learn, see, and do more. Children are very impressionable when they are young, and they learn a lot from what they see. I didn't want Jeremiah to only see the house, medical equipment, and medical professionals. So when he saw lights in the ceiling at a museum, he learned about space, and when he saw animals at a zoo, he learned what kind of species they were. He became intrigued with the animals. We introduced him to reading, and we started with animals and other essential subjects for kids.

Jeremiah even went on a thirty-hour car ride to New York. Yes, he ventured to another city and state. What a great place for him to see the world from a totally different perspective. The road trip was great, and he did well. I quickly learned not to be afraid to venture out and do things like taking long road trips. To this day, he actually loves riding in the car and does so well during long car rides.

While in New York, I took him to Manhattan, and he saw all of the tall buildings. I can honestly say I am not sure what he saw or remembered, but I was happy that I exposed him to it.

A Life Lesson

Don't stop living because you are caring for someone else. When you do that, you limit God's ability to work in your life. God has more for us all, and He will show it to you if you venture out. Laughing, living, and praying are essential if you want to live a full life.

Part 2

Courage

Chapter 7

Trusting My Instincts About My Child

As I stated earlier, Jeremiah was diagnosed with multiple disabilities. He didn't receive his first diagnosis until he was one. He was diagnosed with Triplegic Cerebral Palsy. This meant his legs and left arm were not functioning properly. He wasn't able to walk, and the usage of his left arm and hand was restricted. He could use his right arm and hand. This meant therapies, surgeries, and a continuous, long list of medications.

I took him to see his pediatrician in order to find out how he was developing. During that visit, the pain that I felt when he was born resurfaced. The words shared by medical professionals sounded like the big, loud gongs you hear when the Liberty Bell is rung. Once again, the medical words used didn't make much sense to me, and I didn't quite understand the terms. In addition to cerebral palsy, he was diagnosed with autism, Intellectual Developmental Disability (IDD), and many other medical fragilities. These words were foreign to me, so the doctors had to explain what they meant and the impact they would have on Jeremiah's life.

During this period of his life, I had to learn about the courage that I possessed. I, then, had to use that courage to help him to never give up. I can tell you the road ahead was not looking so bright, and once again, I had to go back to my anchor, which is my relationship with God. Of course, if you were like me, at first, I never wanted to hear a diagnosis because I didn't want to believe that my child had any challenges. Yes, my old acquaintance tried to come and get a natural grip on my heart. My acquaintance's name is "fear." It hit my heart so hard because now, life, as I was hoping it was going to be, looked nothing like how I had imagined it would look.

You have to know all kinds of questions and thoughts entered my head. I started to say, "God, You are a healer, and You can remove all of this from his body." Oh, how I wanted this immediate miracle to take place.

The conversation continued with Jeremiah's doctor, and they shared that, at the early age of four years old, he wouldn't be able to do the following:

- Talk – perhaps could learn some other way to communicate
- Walk – limited to a wheelchair

- Take care of himself

This list noted above was one that I had never ever heard of before. I have seen individuals in life who had a disability, but not one time did I ever think this would happen to me. I know I am not the only person facing a similar situation who ever thought they would hear the news about their child being diagnosed with a disability. Honestly, it took a minute for me to gather up enough strength for us to leave this doctor's appointment.

After leaving the appointment, we headed to Jeremiah's school, where he attended for half-a-day. When I arrived at the school, an administrator and his teacher could see that I had been crying. They asked me what happened, and I shared it with them, and they immediately understood where my tears were coming from. Jeremiah's teacher pulled me aside, looked me in my red eyes, and asked me this one question: "Who do you put all of your trust in?"

I had to dry my face before I could answer. Then, I said, "The Lord!"

She proceeded to say, "Then, what does He say about Jeremiah?"

Boy, that was the best question anyone could

have ever asked me. I didn't take the time to consider asking the One who created him what He had to say about Jeremiah's life. Isn't that just like us when something happens with someone or something? Instead of going back to the manufacturer or creator, we listen to someone else's opinion on a product they never created. Wow! Isn't it amazing how a straightforward question can turn your life around?

Seeing Things Differently

I left Jeremiah at the school because they wanted me to have a moment to myself. I am so glad they did because I had to repent to God and say, "Lord, forgive me for losing sight of what You have promised."

I was taken back to the day when God honored my prayer for Jeremiah's life, and God reminded me that He would take care of him. I also know God showed me a vision for Jeremiah's life, and I didn't see what the doctor described. As a matter of fact, the vision showed Jeremiah talking. The first thing the doctor said, however, was that he wouldn't ever be able to speak.

I recall hearing the doctor explain to me, from a medical perspective, that the brain surgery Jeremiah had when he was one had caused more damage to his brain. During this surgery, they removed a tiny portion of the right side of his brain. This increased the damage to his already damaged brain and created a more advanced stage of cerebral palsy.

After that meeting, I cried out to God and asked what was happening. I asked, "How did you show me a vision of my son talking, when the doctor just told me the exact opposite?"

After moments of me literally crying and doing what sounded like fussing, a still, quiet voice said, "Do you believe what I told you about your son?"

After I regained my composure, I said, "Yes, Lord, I do!" There were no other words for me to say, but "Thank You, Lord."

I had to change my perspective on how I saw Jeremiah and whatever anyone said about him. I had to have the courage to stand on the words that God spoke to me and the Word of God. My vision had to change, and so did my language. I had to come to grips with what I was going to stand on and communicate to others. My eyesight became clear every time I thought about what God had promised me. I can't tell anyone who has a child with a disability not to face what's in front of you, but I can say, "Be sure to seek God." I knew that I only had my faith in God and the courage to believe in the impossible.

When Jeremiah got home from school, all I knew was I had to ask God to help me through this process. He was four and, at this point, had not said a word. Eventually, he turned five, and still no words. There were many birthdays and holidays that I didn't really enjoy. One, in particular, was Mother's Day. People would send me Happy Mother's Day greetings via social media, my phone, email, etc. I didn't like any of them. One day, a friend of mine asked me, "Why don't you like Mother's Day?"

I explained to her that my Mother's Day experience was not the same as other mothers. While I was grateful to be a mother, I told her that my son, at that point, didn't know what Mother's Day was, nor could he say "Happy Mother's Day." When we have children, we look forward to the special occasions that we will celebrate with our children. After I shared that with her, she understood and did everything she could to help me look at things differently.

Subsequently, I finally started seeing the holidays from another viewpoint. I had to constantly remind myself that God is faithful to His promises. I, also, realized that Jeremiah had something that was so extra special to me: his smile.

Even now, it is infectious to everyone that experiences it. He has smiled every day since he came home from the NICU. It didn't matter if he was coming out of surgery or coming home from school; there was a smile on his face. It is the first thing I see each day. That gave me lots of hope that he would smile, no matter how challenging the day was. Something deep down on the inside of me would leap when I saw his smile. I chose to believe that my son had a greater purpose in life. I decided to continue trusting God and pushing ahead. This journey hasn't been easy, but I had to trust that my child would improve and be better, regardless of what anyone said. I had to always lean on my faith in God to know that things would get better and to not be afraid. Thankfully, God had already told me that my son would talk. He'd shown this to me, and I believed Him. And at the age of six, Jeremiah started talking. Yes, he began to use his voice.

A Life Lesson

We call a "gut feeling" our instincts. As mothers, we have to be confident enough to believe in something greater than what we currently see. It takes a lot of courage to believe this way. Know that God will back up whatever He says to you about your child.

Chapter 8
Learning to Exhale

When Jeremiah was about five years old, I came to the conclusion that it was time to learn everything about each of his diagnoses. I needed to understand them so that we could create an action plan for him. The first thing I did was contact all ten of his doctors and ask them to evaluate Jeremiah at this stage in his young life. Then, I asked each one of them, "What steps do we need to take in your area of expertise?"

Each doctor shared their thoughts.

I, then, got with his educational team at his elementary school to see how we would teach him. Finally, I spoke with his therapists and asked them what goals we should set for him. I learned, early on, that the best way to manage everything was to collaborate with the medical team, educational team, and therapy team. The key to Jeremiah's success was *collaboration.* If the same information was not being shared with everyone, we couldn't create the best plan of care for Jeremiah.

I had to spearhead the teams. This was the most efficient strategy to ensure nothing was mishandled. This was a strategy that I used when I was working in Corporate America. It came in handy to ensure Jeremiah received the best care.

A vital component to creating a better life for Jeremiah was listening to everyone's thoughts, based on their expertise. I respected everyone, and they did likewise. I shared with each one that I knew they couldn't tell me Jeremiah's future, but I asked them to look at where he was currently and assess what his needs were. Everyone knew I was going to be very thorough in my approach to managing Jeremiah's care. However, I didn't hesitate to share my perspective as his mother with the experts.

It took a minute for many of them to understand that their word was not the final word on Jeremiah. I wasn't ashamed of my faith in God, and they all knew that played a significant role in what direction we were going to take. Building collaborative teams has been one of the preeminent strategies that I have used to help with Jeremiah's care.

When there was a medical challenge, I would first

contact one of the medical team members. They were great resources. In the earlier years of Jeremiah's life, there were continuous trips to the emergency room at the nearest children's hospital. Jeremiah has had fourteen surgeries within eleven years and countless doctors' appointments. He would, on average, see a hospital between five to six times a month.

As he has gotten older and stronger, the surgeries have lessened, and the ER need has decreased. I am thankful to God for the continuous strengthening of Jeremiah's body. I am ecstatic that Jeremiah has recovered well from all fourteen surgeries. The medical team is pleased as well, and a couple of them have extended the length of time when he needs to come and visit them. This is actual progress.

Openness in the Face of Reality

The many different surgeries that Jeremiah experienced required me to face the physical limitations that he was going through. He required additional assistance because, following the surgeries, he was required to wear leg and hip castings, and the limitations were more significant than usual. This happened when

Jeremiah had his bilateral hip, bilateral gastro lengthening and bilateral ankle tenor lengthening at the same time. The surgery took more than nine hours to complete, and he spent over two weeks in the hospital and came home with casts on both legs.

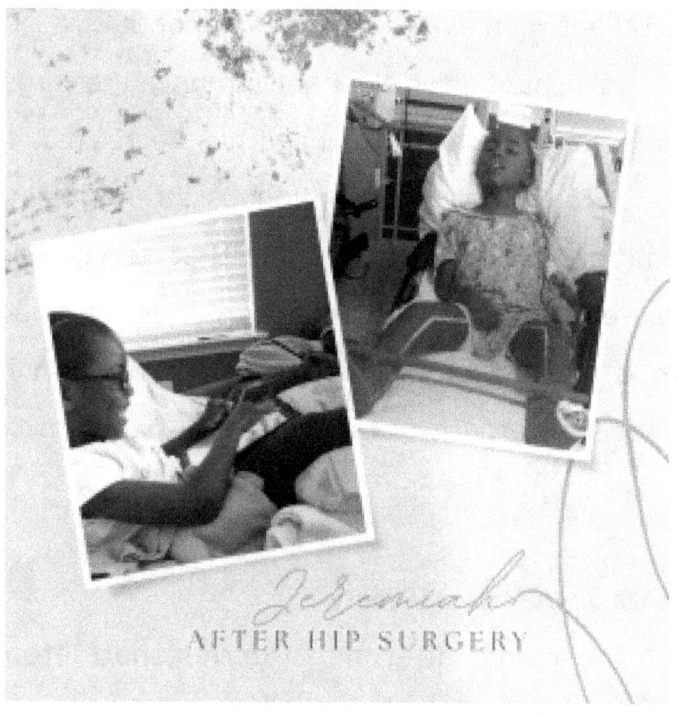

Figure 2. Jeremiah wearing his leg braces.

There was a metal bar holding his legs apart. Jeremiah had to wear this for six or more weeks. Two people were required to lift him because he wasn't able to move his legs at all. When you see your child experiencing these types of massive surgeries, your heart wants to faint each time. There were many sleepless nights and times when my eyes were filled with tears. I felt so helpless, and all I could do was ensure he had the most powerful pain medication to manage his pain level. Because he was not able to verbally communicate, he couldn't tell me how much pain he was in. These were the kind of things that would break my heart. I vacillated between crying and trying to find a way to keep him calm.

During this hospital experience, the doctors forgot to administer daily medication after they completed surgery. Let me be honest. That was one of the most horrific nights of my life. Jeremiah was in excruciating pain, and the way I could tell was he kept crying. The tears ran down his face profusely. I had to have the head of the pain management department and lead doctor figure out a solution to manage Jeremiah's pain.

As his mother, I was angry about the mistake, but my primary focus was to bring it under control. It took several leaders within the hospital to find a way to get Jeremiah's pain managed. I was infuriated by the process, but I didn't back down until there was a resolution. Let's just say that the rest of Jeremiah's two-week stay went very well. Yes, "Mama Bear" came out in full force because I wasn't going to let anyone rest until we fixed this problem. Our children need us to advocate on their behalf and ensure they receive proper care.

Speaking Up Can Change Your Life

As the parent of a child diagnosed with several different disabilities, it is quite apparent that building a support team is essential. You will be the voice for your child, and having a support system helps along the journey. The most complex challenge happens when parents, like me, have to fight big companies and government agencies to receive the appropriate services for our children. The one thing I've learned is that I cannot be afraid to speak up for my child. Every parent caring for a child with disabilities has a right to speak up on behalf of their child. Sometimes, parents are afraid of what others may think, and they do not know how to speak up. I can empathize with them because I understand. However, I also know that I have to constantly advocate for my son.

After I began to learn about the rights my child had as a citizen of the USA, I realized that, sometimes, people didn't want to recognize the uniqueness of my child. Even though two children might have the same or similar diagnoses, this may not equate to them needing the same services. I learned it was my responsibility to be Jeremiah's voice. It didn't matter if a large corporation didn't want to service him or if the educational system tried to limit him. Throughout this book, the one consistent throughline has been that I seek God's wisdom and stand on His Word concerning Jeremiah's life. This has been and will always be my anchor for every decision I make concerning Jeremiah.

The challenges are many, and they vary from season to season and, sometimes, even day-to-day. The most interesting aspect that I've seen as the caregiver of someone who has been diagnosed with a disability is that I have had to learn to adapt to their style of communicating. The brain damage Jeremiah experienced has caused some blockages in areas that create challenges when it comes to fully understanding his

FAITH - COURAGE - GRACE

immediate needs. Most of what I have learned is from the medical team and from researching a particular diagnosis. Ironically, each of the disabilities has an enormous amount of different aspects. They usually reference it as the spectrum or umbrella, which means many variables that have the same name.

Acquiring an understanding of these various diagnoses is not an easy task, and it is one that I am still learning. As our children grow, things change even within the diagnosis, and of course, their needs do, too. Learning is a critical characteristic of caring for someone diagnosed with a disability. As Jeremiah matures, helping him to better understand what is happening with him is another aspect for me to keep in mind. It takes a lot of courage and strength to walk alone in this journey. Many times, parents lose sight of what's important because they become weary and downright tired.

This is nothing to be ashamed of, and even as a solid Christian, we all get weary. I know I get that way many times and have to speak up and say to someone, "I need help." Honestly, that was the biggest challenge for me personally because I'd always felt it was my responsibility to take care of all his needs on my own.

122

Well, time caught up with me, and so did my age. I am very grateful for my daughter, who has been there through many of the ups and downs with me. However, one essential thing was for her to finish her education. And she did! She received her master's degree in special education. She is working on her second master's in autism spectrum disorder.

I believe it is crucial that we ask for help when we need it and embrace it when it comes. Jeremiah is the one who gets the very best of it all. He gets to know another person, and it gives me time to get some rest. There should be a prescription written from a doctor that requires caregivers to get a certain amount of rest per month. Without hesitation, I would go fill that prescription.

A Life Lesson

Listening to others and learning about your child will only benefit you in the long run. It gives you the wisdom that you will need to help make sure you are on the right path. Don't be afraid to speak up because it can change everyone's lives for the better. God Himself said to ask, so we shouldn't be afraid to ask others for help.

Chapter 9

Courage Takes Lots of Practice

When you are facing something beyond your control, it takes lots of courage to keep on living. I didn't realize the amount of courage it would take to face hearing a whole lot of things that would repeatedly break my heart about the person I gave birth to. All parents want healthy children. No one expects to have a child with a disability. When it does happen, life can change immediately, and it can look completely different than it did before our precious child was born.

In cases like mine, after having Jeremiah, I was taken to a different place as a parent. As a result, I have had to process life differently. Many people don't understand the unending psychological battle that we parents have to wage every day. Daily, I wonder if I can do anything to better my child's life or if I am doing enough to meet all of his needs, so he can live his best life. Over time, it helps to be honest with yourself about exactly where you are at that moment.

It's hard to describe the types of mental and emotional challenges that we face as parents. There have been times when I start crying as I look at my child in a public place and see how other children are running around with ease and not a care in the world. Meanwhile, here is my son in a wheelchair, wanting to do the same things as the other children.

It is often challenging to have these types of conversations with others because they will say, "I understand exactly what you're going through."

When people say this, I know they are trying to be empathetic. But I have stopped people and asked, "How do you understand what I am experiencing?"

It is a blunt question, but in reality, nobody truly understands. You may have some empathy for a parent, but words are powerful and how we express them is most important. Even though I am on this journey, I could not say to another parent in a similar situation that I understand. The most effective thing you can do is to listen and ask how you can help. But only if you are sincere.

Many people say they want to help but don't know what to do. Whenever I would ask someone to watch Jeremiah, they would be afraid because they didn't know how to connect to Jeremiah or children like him. I believe they genuinely wanted to help but were too afraid to ask difficult questions. It is better to ask those questions so that you can learn how you can help.

Many people who see Jeremiah while he's sitting in his wheelchair notice that he rocks back and forth. There is always an inquisitive look on their faces. They also see that he has a large scar on his head. Honestly, the stares happen many times, especially when other children are around.

Some people don't understand that he's a child and wants to be treated as one. He likes when others engage with him. If you speak to Jeremiah, he is going to speak back to you. Asking me, his parent, the best way to connect with my child could get you started on the right path. When there are other children around, Jeremiah lights up.

At the age of one, Jeremiah had to have brain surgery to remove a growing cyst. The ironic part of this was that the cyst was growing in an area of the brain that had no life in it. When his surgeon went in to remove it, she immediately realized that it had grown in size. Interestingly, the cyst was discovered in February, and by September, it had almost doubled in size. So Jeremiah had surgery. Following the surgery, the scar remained, and many people think that it is a shunt, but it is scaring from the brain surgery. So this scar added to the physical image of how people saw Jeremiah and why they were hesitant to engage with him.

Consider, for a moment, if you were in my shoes as a parent. How would you feel if people you knew kept their distance from you because they didn't know how to connect to your child?

Losing relationships is a common thing for parents like me. I have experienced that, and it does hurt, especially when people know that you have challenges and don't even ask how you are doing. It takes a lot of courage to get up and keep a smile on my face, especially when life changes from minute to minute. Things have gotten better, but finding help hasn't been easy. This is when I prayed to God, asking that He sends the right people into our lives, people who genuinely love all people. If you look at Jeremiah as if something is wrong, it will be difficult for you to be in his presence.

Remember, all children are perceptive and can tell when you are real or not. All children like to watch cartoons, play games, and read. Many times, it's all about finding what a child likes; for example, Mickey Mouse is a universal cartoon character that most children like. Perhaps reading a book would help you connect with children like Jeremiah. Honestly, Jeremiah loves to be read to, and yes, he loves Mickey Mouse.

Another universal area of interest is music. Most children love to listen to music or sing songs. It takes courage and bravery to engage with families that have someone with a disability.

I know this journey has many difficulties, and having support makes a world of difference. Knowing there is someone out there thinking about us is equally as important. As Christians, we are supposed to bear each other's burdens and show God's love to all, even those who live life differently or who may not comm-unicate in the same manner we do. I constantly pray to God for others to come along with me on this journey and show themselves to be friendly. This is not a cry for pity because that is the most insulting thing someone could ever feel for my son and me. Most parents believe that, if people know how amazing our children are, there would be no way they could pity them. Many of our children grow up to become influential contributors to society, so pity would be devastating to a family, especially to that child because someone like Jeremiah only sees life from the perspective that he entered it. He doesn't compare himself to others, and he doesn't hope to become someone else; instead, he hopes to become the best person he can be.

The most interesting thing to keep in mind, if you are a Christian, is that we were ALL made in the image of God. Wow! What does that mean? It simply means that God has some disabilities as well. If not, then it would mean that only some are made in His image. I don't recall it saying that anywhere in the Bible. It is easy for me to see God in Jeremiah. Trust me, if you ever got to know Him, you would echo my sentiments as well. I know it is not an easy road to be on, but I wouldn't change anything. I believe God gives us situations to bring out the very best in us. Jeremiah certainly is bringing the best out in me and how I view life.

Strength Along the Journey

There have been so many days when I have

looked at this journey I have been on and seen where I have acquired the strength to remain courageous. Even after a few days of emotional drainage and being mentally worn out, something always enters my mind to remind me how valuable I am. It takes strength from within that God has given me that I cannot explain to anyone else.

As a single mother, raising Jeremiah, I've learned that I have so much more strength from within. I didn't know how much God would give me, but He has given me the capacity to handle all of this and not faint. Yes, I have had to seek out tools and resources to help myself, but knowing to tap into them was critical. What kind of tools are there?

I recommend going to counseling. It is an effective tool. Counseling allows you to speak to someone who is neutral who can help you keep the proper perspective. When those moments of feeling overwhelmed seem unending, speaking with a counselor is a great way to obtain perspective and strength. Do not ever think that asking for help is weak. It takes courage to seek out help. It is not anything to be ashamed of, and I strongly encourage others to do it.

Five years ago, I started going to counseling because I recognized I needed some help. It took courage to admit that I needed help. I had to realize that I was not losing faith in God by seeking out help. It has aided me in bouncing back faster when the tough days are too much.

Let's fast forward to Jeremiah's life and what it can look like. This is only a sample. Jeremiah has grown tall and still wears pull-ups. Now, I still have to lift him to get him ready each day, and I have to administer all of his daily medications that range between nine to fourteen and above.

Jeremiah and I currently live in a place that has stairs. This means that he has to be transported up and down the stairs to his wheelchair. He still needs assistance with dressing, bathing, grooming, etc. Of course, Jeremiah has to eat, and he needs assistance with feeding as well. Every time he leaves the house, he gets into the car, which means another lift, and the wheelchair has to be disassembled and put into the car. These are just his daily basic needs. They don't include taking him to doctor or therapy appointments.

When he goes out in public, we have to make

sure there is accessibility for him to enjoy his surroundings without having a meltdown. Oh, yeah, meltdowns can occur at any time and in any place. He doesn't have control over them.

Another thing to consider is getting myself ready for the day. It takes lots of strength and patience to make it through any given day.

Once the day ends, getting him prepared for bed is a whole additional process that requires bathing, medications, and other things for him to sleep. Many aspects of a typical day haven't been mentioned because the list is too long.

A Life Lesson

God will give you the courage and strength for each day as you seek His face. Be honest and open to receiving help and even ask God to bring the right people into your life. God sees everything and will strengthen you and give you the courage to keep walking along the journey.

Part 3

Grace

Chapter 10

When It Hurts Too Much to Pray

Pain Beyond the Pain that's Covered by Grace

For me, a new way of life began upon Jeremiah's birth, upon hearing the things that gripped my heart so tight that they caused my mind to wonder, How am I going to make it? I often think back to the first moments after I received Jeremiah's initial medical diagnosis and, later, the full list of what Jeremiah would not be able to do.

Candidly, those words have never left my mind, and they certainly haven't left my heart. After learning that words have life and death, it became essential for me not to allow the words to define my circumstance. Jeremiah has been told so many negative things that, if I permitted them to stay in my heart or mind, I would be in a constant state of pain. I truly believe that God wants us to give Him all of our pain. He stated in His Word in 1 Peter 5:7 (NLT) to "give all your worries and cares to God" because He cares for us.

When I was speaking with a medical doctor who I trusted to provide me with, as best as they could, an accurate account of what was happening to my son Jeremiah, the doctor opened their mouth to tell me the many limitations they saw for Jeremiah and how that would impact my life. My first reaction was, this can't be true. A strong sense of denial happened, and then my ears and mind opened up again to what was in front of me. The next few moments, and even days, had so many emotional and mental challenges that, many times, I didn't know if I was coming or going. Yes, I immediately wanted to yell at God. I wanted to know why this was happening to me. But truthfully, I didn't do that because I knew that pain happens in life, and I had to decide how I would respond to it.

Prayer is the next and most important thing that comes to my mind. At that time, it didn't look like what many people would consider prayer. I removed any formal ways of talking to God, like getting on my knees and reciting certain words to get God's attention.

Here's how it went for me. I fell out on the floor, crying my heart out, asking God, "How am I going to make it?"

All of my cares were being communicated to God in my tears and a few words. There came a moment when the crying slowed down and my words began to take over. I talked to God from my heart, and I believed He heard me. Did anything change immediately?

No, but I felt better after opening up and being very transparent with God. My prayer time or, as I would say, "crying time" became a daily routine. The kicking and screaming at God didn't produce much for me other than a headache. What did help was the crying because, even without words, God still heard me. That's the one thing that I am learning. Tears express a lot to God, especially when you don't know what else to do. I eventually cried less and talked more. Please know that tears still exist and will continue because it hurts to hear things that I didn't want to hear. My prayer time with God helped me to better handle the things that were too painful for me to handle. I had to learn how to give all of my pain to God.

Let's have an open and transparent conversation about giving all of our pain or cares to God. It's a process. This doesn't mean it's not possible; it means that it isn't always a straight and easy road to success. How often have you said that you're giving something over to God in your prayer time while crying out to God?

Then, no sooner than you finish that prayer, you discover yourself trying to figure out what you can do to fix or change the circumstances. As human beings, I believe that we can convince ourselves that we are giving our cares and pains to God, but in reality, we are simply saying lots of words. I believe we have very good intentions when we pray that we want God to take the pain away. It becomes challenging when I keep seeing things the same way I did before I prayed, especially when I take Jeremiah to a doctor or have a meeting at his school and hear another negative report. Despite what I listen to others say, I have to keep reminding myself about what God has to say.

Additionally, I must do my best to say what God says, no matter what I am seeing or experiencing. That sounds crazy or foreign to some, but it is what we born-again believers call "faith." Hebrews 11:1 (NLT) states that "Faith shows the reality of what we hope for; it is the evidence of things we cannot see." I've had to decide, many times along the way, to keep my faith in God. It gave me a determination not to give up and to keep moving forward. Emotionally, I had many challenges. Mentally, I had many challenges, and spiritually, I had many challenges. I share this to paint a clear picture that this is an ongoing process. I continue to learn how to pace myself so that I don't become so overwhelmed, thinking I can't move or accomplish anything. This will negatively affect Jeremiah and me.

Another Way of Thinking

After adopting a life of faith, it became pretty apparent that I needed some divine assistance. I had to be honest with myself. I had to understand that grace was what God was giving me. As each day, month, and year has gone by, Jeremiah's life has had many obstacles, but I had a choice to make each time. I could either get overwhelmed with the hurt, disappointment, and other negative feelings, or I could understand that I was experiencing God's grace. It was my decision to encounter God's grace and allow virtue to come directly from God. I had to shift my thinking about Jeremiah's life and how I would handle the many things we faced.

Whenever the pain or hurt would become too great, I would have to pause and ask for God's grace to be with me continually. I often thought I understood God's grace and how I thought it would show up in my life. Along this journey, I gleaned that God's life, power, and righteousness were given to us by His unmerited favor. All this meant was that God showed me that His love and kindness were mine, based on me giving my life to Him. Because I gave my life to God, it is grace that He extends to me continually.

I've grown to value and appreciate having God's grace with an understanding that it's not based on anything I did or didn't do. It is simply God's way of showing His kindness through the death and resurrection of Jesus Christ for all of my sins. Having this exposed to me has helped to transform my life and Jeremiah's life. It doesn't mean that challenges and heartaches stopped in Jeremiah's life; it simply means that I have confidence that God is with us both.

Once I began to shift my thinking, whenever I heard another negative report, I knew I had grown because I began to receive the information differently. To this current day, I still receive adverse reports from my son's medical team, educational team, and even within his community. I must always examine how and what I think after I hear these negative words about Jeremiah. As a mother, I can't stop fighting or growing because something has changed. We have to continue the same thing I shared earlier in this book about bringing everything to God openly and honestly.

Don't be afraid to ask for additional help to hold you up during those difficult times. One thing that has helped and will continue to help is building a stronger and closer relationship with God. I am continuously learning how to accept God's grace and how to find ways to align my thinking with whatever God has said.

A Life Lesson

Don't allow the hurt or pain from a tragedy or tragic circumstances cause you to become despondent. Giving God all of your hurts and pains is what He wants. Allow God's grace into your life to lift you up because He freely gives to you through His finished work on the cross. God's grace is never earned, but it will sustain you through the most challenging times of your life.

Chapter 11
Unpredictable Emotions

The Truth and Nothing but the Truth

When God speaks to me, I take it as truth. God confirmed for me, after declaring that Jeremiah would not die, that he would live to declare the works of the Lord. The truth is that, in order to declare something, you have to speak it out of your mouth. I was told numerous times that Jeremiah would never be able to talk due to the brain damage he experienced at birth. The truth is, at this current time, Jeremiah is able to read out loud and above his grade level. His is a voice that I love to hear whenever he watches a cartoon that he loves. This is when he's talking back to the TV or iPad. He recites several chapters in the Bible daily, and he can mock me very well.

If you recall, I shared earlier how I didn't like Mother's Day. Now, with his extraordinary voice, he says, "Happy Mother's Day," "Happy Birthday," "Merry Christmas," and even "open up the presents." Despite those early medical and educational reports, Jeremiah is speaking. God is still healing his speech. Currently, he has some challenges with expressive language. However, no matter the challenges we are currently facing, it is fantastic to hear Jeremiah reading, spelling, and reciting words.

Interestingly, when Jeremiah started talking, his teachers and therapists were all very shocked. His medical team was astonished, as well. The one thing I did consistently was always speak clearly to him so that he would hear how words were annunciated. It was the Lord teaching me to never stop using my words when speaking to Jeremiah. I would remind Jeremiah continuously that I believed he had a voice. It was challenging because, for years, there was no evidence of his voice. However, when he turned six years old, words flowed out of his mouth.

Oh, Happy Days

If you don't see anything changing, it can be very challenging to believe or have faith as a born-again believer. It was tough to have medical professionals show me X-rays or MRI results that proved why they believed Jeremiah wouldn't speak. I respect Jeremiah's medical team and have built excellent working relationships with them. So, I never wanted anyone to think I wasn't listening to their medical advice or expertise. It was the direct opposite; I listened intently. Then, I would pray. My faith in God continues to anchor and govern how I care for Jeremiah.

The doctors all said that they were happy to hear Jeremiah speaking. The one thing I can say about all of his doctors is that none of them ever said that what they said was the absolute final truth. They were all just sharing based on the medical evidence and the type of brain damage Jeremiah experienced.

It was a very happy day when I could go to a doctor's appointment, and Jeremiah either read to the doctor or answered the doctor's questions. One of the happiest days was when I took Jeremiah to an eye exam, and whenever the doctor asked what letter he could see, Jeremiah answered all of the questions himself. His doctor had the biggest smile on his face when he heard Jeremiah tell him precisely what he was seeing. There were so many happy days because Jeremiah was able to respond.

Even though Jeremiah currently has expressive

language challenges, he's still improving. His therapists adjust their methods to help him improve. They shared that Jeremiah's receptive language is good; however, his expressive language will still need additional work. Limited expressive language is when someone is challenged with expressing their feelings, pain, or emotions. I will continue to stand on the promises of God and provide Jeremiah with the resources he needs.

Jeremiah's journey, thus far, has had various challenges and many victories. God has either told me or shown me many things that will take place in a vision, and I believe they will all come to pass. One of the essential things is not trying to figure out how it will come to pass. I have a responsibility to only believe in and have faith in God. He's responsible for bringing what He promises to manifestation. This doesn't mean that I do absolutely nothing; instead, what I do is constantly seek out God for His direction. How the promises become fulfilled is not up to any of us; it is all up to God.

It is human nature to want to help God out by bringing His promises to life. Ironically, God knows that about us, and He patiently waits for us to relinquish our need for control.

The beautiful thing about God is that He created us and knows us better than we know ourselves. I have to remember that nothing about Jeremiah or me is new to God. What God wants is for every believer to trust in and rely on Him for everything. When we accept His grace, we recognize that He is in complete control of whatever He has promised or said would happen. That sounds really easy to process; however, in reality, it is very challenging for me. I'm very grateful for God's grace because it helps me when I have everything together and going in the right direction. His grace also covers me when I mess everything up and go in the wrong direction. We serve a God who loves providing us with His favor and divine assistance in our lives. Knowing this simple fact helps to make many of my days happy ones.

A Life Lesson

You can depend on whatever God has promised you. Without question, He will bring every promise into manifestation for your life. Always know that God's grace is freely given to us and believe that He will honor what He has said to you about your life and your circumstances.

Chapter 12
Grace that Conquers

Sacrifices that Build Strength

Even though I am Jeremiah's mother, I am also his caregiver. What does that mean, and why is that even important? I didn't realize that, while raising my son who has received multiple disability diagnoses, I would have so much on my plate.

Reflecting on the time he first came home from the NICU until now, the caregiving aspect means I have to do everything for him. It's crucial because no mother plans on changing a pull-up or dressing their child up until the age of eight and even beyond. Each day, mothers teach their children how to take care of themselves, so their children can become less dependent on them and more independent. When you transition from mother to caregiver, you are the one doing most of the tasks. It is a huge sacrifice because I must think about my son's needs before thinking about mine. God has given me the strength to take care of those needs and has helped me along the way.

Honestly, caregiving is one of the most challenging difficulties that I face because I want to make sure my son is good at all times. However, as a mother, I want to see him learn to take care of himself. Having to lift him up to move him everywhere he needs to be, dress him, and assist him with feeding can be emotionally draining. Interestingly, God is building strength in me while I am caring for Jeremiah. I am not going to paint a picture that caregiving is something that I ever wanted to do, but because I know that God has trusted me to do this, I will do it as unto God.

While I care for Jeremiah, I often have tears streaming down my face or am completely exhausted. Somehow, God gives me the strength for each day and helps me get up the next day and do it all over again. Jeremiah is who God gave me because, even if I don't feel good, God gives me my daily dosages of strength to get through any given day. Additionally, God is teaching me so much about who He is through Jeremiah's life.

At all times, Jeremiah is very loving. If you ask Jeremiah how he is feeling, he will tell you he's feeling happy. He doesn't complain and only wants my love, time, and attention. He likes for me to intentionally focus on him. He never stops smiling, not even in difficult or painful situations. He can calm anyone and have you feeling at peace. Whenever I am having a challenging day, spending time with Jeremiah instantly changes my perspective. His love is unconditional, and he enjoys bringing joy to others in his unique way. Whenever you encounter him, spending even just a few minutes with Jeremiah almost guarantees that you will look at life from a different and positive perspective.

God's loving grace gives me the strength I need to keep me forging ahead in life. As I mentioned earlier, I vacillate between many different emotions; however, I look to God to strengthen me when I am weak.

Deep within Shows

When I recognize these different emotions, the grace within shows. Conquering each of these challenges reveals what was deep down on the inside of me. It's funny how, when life squeezes you so tight, you begin to see what's really on the inside of you. Within one day, I can wear several hats. I can go from being a mother with so much uncertainty to a caregiver who has to rely on God's wisdom to make daily decisions. Finally, I am a person who, through the grace of God, is able to help others at a moment's notice. Sometimes, I have to switch these roles from one moment to the next. And I recognize that this is a lifelong journey. I don't get to exit this ride just because I am having a hard day. Ironically, throughout all of these obstacles and while not clearly understanding why this has happened to me, I saw that my heart revealed itself when I reflected on this entire journey. Even as believers in God, we can, sometimes, not see all of the good in situations. For me, several things became abundantly clear when I realized that God had more for me beyond what I was facing.

In pure transparency, for years, I thought my life was pretty much going to only focus on being a single mother and caregiver. How wrong I was. I forgot that God always has a plan. Even if I didn't see one, God opened me up to other possibilities through my willingness to do things afraid.

Jeremiah, along the way, took a strong liking to Mickey Mouse. He enjoyed watching the *Mickey Mouse Clubhouse* and everything Mickey. As a mother, I asked

God to bless us with a trip to Disney World. Our God is so faithful. When we ask, He answers. He blessed us with a phenomenal trip to Disney World that changed a lot of perspectives that I had acquired. It exposed me to the simple fact that Jeremiah can still enjoy life similar to other children. Think for a moment. I had to take into account that Jeremiah was in a wheelchair and that he had a sensitivity to sounds. Because of his many medical challenges, he was either going to the ER or a doctor's appointment within any week. It appeared as if traveling was not an option for him.

Oh, how wrong I was about what Jeremiah would be able to do. When we experienced Disney World, it was the best time ever. Disney provides outstanding customer service and support. We got to experience all the parks and get on as many rides as we wanted. They had an exceptional process for those living with a disability. Disney has trained their staff on how to treat all park attendees with respect and dignity. That experience revealed a deep passion of mine, which is giving to others. After we had such a good time, it was my heart's desire to help other families caring for someone living with disabilities go on a vacation to

Disney.

I was approaching my fiftieth birthday and decided to bless a family with a trip to Disney World. Of course, the question that immediately came to my mind was, How in the world can I do this? Whenever God places something deep within my heart, He always provides the means to support that passion.

Jeremiah has been and continues to be my inspiration in life. He inspired me to launch a non-profit that would help families caring for someone with a disability. I decided to call it Jeremiah's Voice. The name came from a discussion I had with a friend, and she suggested that name. Our motto is "Living Beyond Disability." I genuinely believe that there is still life, even after a medical diagnosis, and I wanted to give others hope and inspiration by allowing them to have some fun.

Launching Jeremiah's Voice was the most incredible feeling because of what we set as a goal, and we achieved it. A family did go on a five-days/four-nights all-expense paid vacation on behalf of Jeremiah's Voice. As an organization, we decided that we would celebrate the lives of those living with a disability, caring for someone living with a disability, or supporting the disability community. We have three core values that help us support others.

One of our core values is we provide *life enrichment*. This simply means we enrich the lives of the families and individuals with disabilities by equipping them to live a more fulfilled life beyond their disabilities. Moms' retreats and support resources are just a few of the events and programs we provide to specifically enrich lives.

Another core value is *we celebrate lives*. It is our belief that we should celebrate the lives of those living with disabilities, caregivers, educators, medical professionals and community supporters. During our Celebrate Life event, we enjoy giving away vacations and other outstanding awards.

The other core value is our *Hope for the Holidays* initiative. Annually, during Christmas, we provide a fully catered meal and age-specific and disability-appropriate gifts to families.

Each of our core values allows us to impact children, adults, parents and caregivers in ways that help them to *live beyond disability*. While living life as a parent/caregiver, you can get so caught up in taking care of your child that you forget how to live. Jeremiah's Voice was created to bring hope and inspiration so that parents/caregivers can see beyond a to-do list, organizing doctors' or therapy appointments, or coordinating transportation and dealing with the educational system.

As a mother, I have to be honest for, at least, six years I felt like my life had stopped, and I didn't know how to teach Jeremiah there was more to life. Each time we try something we want to share it with others to let them know that they can do it. Jeremiah's Voice is the vehicle through which we can do that for others.

Jeremiah's Voice, Inc. is a 501 (c)3 public charity that serves families caring for someone with a disability. We believe that helping others is part of being a born-again believer, and you can do it within the church and outside of the church. As the founder of Jeremiah's Voice, it was purposeful that it be set up as a public charity, so that we can serve anyone who is parenting or caregiving for someone living with a disability. Honestly, disability has no limitation on who can be impacted, so as an organization, we want to bring that hope and inspiration to as many as we can.

At the launch event for Jeremiah's Voice, to see the looks on the child and his brother's face when they found out they'd just won a trip to Disney brought all of the birthday joy I ever needed. We are growing as an organization and helping more families in order to let them know that they are not forgotten. I can't tell you how many times I've heard another parent say that they never thought they would ever be considered for receiving anything, let alone the trips, food, or gifts. They've told me that it felt good for them to know that someone out there cares. When they learn that I am a parent just like them, it brings strength and encouragement.

Jeremiah's Voice continues to build relationships with companies, other non-profits, schools, and the community at large. We believe in collaborations because they have a greater impact within the disability community. We are strategic in how we partner with others because we always want to see it be a win-win relationship. We are here to raise awareness, build tolerance and sensitivity, and foster a community that embraces differences.

I have a heart for giving to others, and along this journey, I discovered this is one of my passions in life. The joyful feeling I get from knowing that I am helping others live lives beyond a diagnosis of a disability helps me greatly appreciate the path my life has taken. What God has placed on the inside of me shows that He has had this trait within me all my life. It takes grace to expose the genuine nuggets that only God can give because giving is a direct reflection of the character of God.

When I was a child, God placed giving within me, but life covered it with many trials and tribulations. It is just like God to expose it and bring life to it when I was experiencing a difficult time in life.

The grace of God has taught me so many valuable lessons and enriched my walk with Him. I can look at raising Jeremiah from a place of victory, not defeat, because God knew that I would grow closer to Him. From the beginning of Jeremiah's life, I immediately learned that I was not in control, nor was I ever going to be in control. I continue to realize that my dependency is only on God to truly help me along the way.

Victory by Grace

There were many times I wanted to remain angry, hurt, and bitter about this journey. However, while walking with God, I have to recognize that He didn't make a mistake by bring me along this pathway. By His divine assistance and grace, I enjoy each day that He gives me.

Over the last ten years, I can honestly say there have been so many victories. I am stronger than I've ever been in my walk with God. I have grown and can appreciate the intimacy I have with God. I have an attitude of gratefulness, not one of regret. This doesn't mean I wanted Jeremiah to experience this many diverse challenges. Still, it means that having God with us makes it worth it. Victory doesn't always equate to my circumstances changing entirely, but my perspective and relationship with God has increased. I've taken a hard and long look at myself and asked myself if I would have as close of a walk with God as I do today. My honest answer is I don't believe so. Of course, this is based on my finite mind, but God's infinite purpose and plan have prevailed.

When I look back and examine everything, I

realize that Jeremiah's entry into the world pushed me into a place I'd never been. I was transferred to a path that would take me directly to Christ. One of the most significant victories was when I placed my faith in God and stood on His Word. It was then that I knew God was more than what I have read or preached or heard about. It is a victorious experience to cleave to God and continue to grow with God taking the lead. Jeremiah's life has shown me clearly that, no matter what I face, God will always teach me who He is and show His plan. I had to relinquish everything to God so that I could see the victories throughout this journey. God sees everything about Jeremiah and me. He will continue to give us His grace to conquer the apparent obstacles that come along with caregiving.

A Life Lesson

Once you open up to God and allow Him to reveal to you that He knows what's on the inside of you, it becomes easier to look to God for everything. Hold on to the understanding that, whatever we face, God will bring out of you what He has placed deep inside that will bring Him glory.

Conclusion

When we are faced with obstacles and challenges that we never thought would happen, it is then that God can teach us and help us to grow in a deeper relationship with Him. Whatever we experience in this life does not take God by surprise, and He desires to walk with us along the way. I've learned the power of forgiveness from multiple aspects. The primary element of forgiveness is I know God has forgiven me and loves me unconditionally. Another part of forgiveness is forgiving when we have been deeply hurt by someone. In this case, it was Jeremiah's father. I've learned that forgiving him helped me grow, and it opened my heart to allow God to step in. Whatever pain, disappointment, hurt, or challenge you are experiencing, remember that God wants to be there for you. I will repeatedly say that all situations can be handled and nurtured by our loving God. Even if we created the problem, He wants to take it and help us walk through it.

It took **Faith** to believe in Jeremiah's life from the very beginning. It has taken **Courage** to never give up on him or myself. It is the ultimate **Grace** of God that will sustain and encourage me to know God is for me. We've walked this far along the journey, and only God knows what's ahead for Jeremiah and me. The one critical component is that I now look to God for His leadership and His guidance so that I can honor Him with my life.

God made me more promises regarding Jeremiah's life, and I will stand on what He revealed to me about Jeremiah. With the help of the good Lord, I will not lose faith in what God has shown me about Jeremiah's future. I always remember God takes delight in offering His power and strength in our weakness. Jeremiah's life will become exactly what God said from the first day of His life. I will testify continually as it unfolds. I trust God and look totally to Him for every step that we need and should take. God, thank you for teaching us all that You love us despite ourselves. God, I am honored to be your daughter.

FAITH - COURAGE - GRACE

When Giving Birth Doesn't Go as Planned, You Find a Way to Live

A Personal Invitation to All Readers

If you have not yet established a personal relationship with Christ, I want to introduce or re-introduce you to Christ. If you have fallen away from God because life happens, I want to introduce you or re-introduce you to Christ. If you have been angry with God because someone you loved dearly has left you through death or separation, I want to introduce you or re-introduce you to Christ. If you think God doesn't love you, I want to introduce you or re-introduce you to Christ. If you have done something that you feel is so horrible that God won't forgive you, I want to introduce you or re-introduce you to Christ. If you are tired of life for whatever reason, I want to introduce or re-introduce you to Christ.

No matter where you are in life, praying this simple prayer will bring you immediately into the right relationship with Christ. **As you read this prayer, say it out loud, so you can hear it:**

Lord, Jesus, I ask you to forgive me of my sins, and I ask you to come into my heart. Lord, I openly declare that Jesus is Lord, and I believe in my heart that God raised Him from the dead, and according to Your Word, I am saved! Thank you, Lord, for saving me, and I also ask You to be Lord over my life and lead me along the path that You have planned for me, in Jesus' name. Amen!

Welcome into the Family of God!

About the Author

Jacquie A. McIver is a speaker, philanthropist, and author. She is a born-again believer of Jesus Christ and committed to sharing the love of God with others. In *Faith-Courage-Grace: When Giving Birth Doesn't Go As Planned, You Find a Way to Live*, Jacquie beautifully writes about how the birth of her son helped her recommit to God. Her writing is raw, honest, and transparent. There is an urgency to her writing that leaves readers breathless. Her real-life story provides personal details about how a devastating prognosis of multiple disabilities for her baby boy completely transformed her relationship with God, and made her a victor, and not just a survivor. Her frank testimony about how the power of faith, courage, and grace spared her life and her sanity, and strengthened her steadfast belief that he still has a chance at life, is both empowering and uplifting for readers experiencing the same circumstances. She shares her poignant testimony from her earliest days as a new mother. She had to shoulder the heart-wrenching news from doctors that her son would be born with life-altering disabilities. Her style is raw, riveting, and relatable for parents who are having to make tough decisions about their child's quality of life.

Jacquie's willingness to share with her readers what she's learned along the way, from the devastating prognosis of her son at birth to her present role as his mother, will provide disheartened parents with renewed hope, counsel, and wisdom. She leaves her readers and those who place this book in the hands of parents or guardians of special needs children, or anyone who may be facing life-altering challenges with the message that, with faith, courage, and grace, a devastating doctor's report, doesn't equate to a life that has to be lived without hope. In other words, she has faced it, lived it, triumphed in it, and found that, in spite of it all, *"You can find a way to live!"*

Jacquie is the President and Founder of Jeremiah's Voice, Inc., a 501 (c)3 public charity. Jeremiah's Voice brings inspiration and hope to hundreds of families caring for children or adults with special needs by celebrating lives, strengthening support systems, and equipping families for living a fulfilled life beyond their disabilities. Currently, Jacquie resides in Texas with her beloved son Jeremiah and adult god-daughter Iesha.

To stay connected with Jacquie:

www.JacquieMcIver.com
Facebook: @jacquieamciver
Instagram: @jacquie.mciver

Jeremiah's Voice, Inc.

Our Core Values

➤ We Provide Life Enrichment
➤ We Celebrate Lives
➤ We Bring Hope for the Holidays

To support us, go to:

www.JeremiahsVoice.org

We are a 501 (c) 3 public charity that strives to be the voice of inspiration and hope for parents/caregivers of children and adults with disabilities.